TAROT
in
MOTION

TAROT
in
MOTION

A Handbook to
Embody Wisdom
through the Cards

MIRIAM JACOBS

REDFeather™

MIND | BODY | SPIRIT

4880 Lower Valley Road, Atglen, PA 19310

Cover and interior design by Ashley Millhouse
Type set in Garamond/Avenir Next

ISBN: 978-0-7643-6175-3
Printed in India

Disclaimer:
The FDA has not evaluated the information in this book. It is not medical or psychological advice. It is not meant to cure or prevent disease. Please consult a medical doctor or psychotherapist for such information.
For privacy reasons some of the names in the quotes are incomplete or changed.

Published by REDFeather Mind, Body, Spirit
An imprint of Schiffer Publishing, Ltd.
4880 Lower Valley Road
Atglen, PA 19310
Phone: (610) 593-1777; Fax: (610) 593-2002
E-mail: Info@redfeathermbs.com
Web: www.redfeathermbs.com

For our complete selection of fine books on this and related subjects, please visit our website at www.redfeathermbs.com. You may also write for a free catalog.

REDFeather Mind Body Spirit's titles are available at special discounts for bulk purchases for sales promotions or premiums. Special editions, including personalized covers, corporate imprints, and excerpts, can be created in large quantities for special needs. For more information, contact the publisher.

We are always looking for people to write books on new and related subjects. If you have an idea for a book, please contact us at proposals@schifferbooks.com.

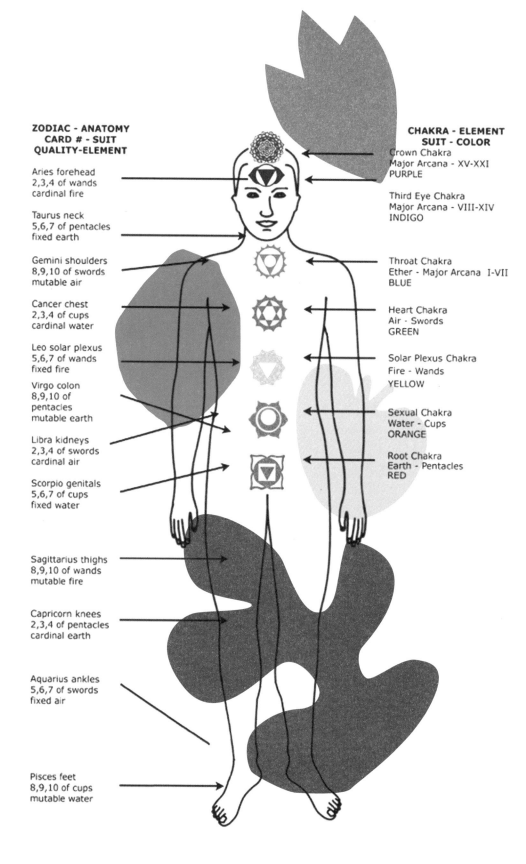

ZODIAC - ANATOMY
CARD # - SUIT
QUALITY-ELEMENT

Aries forehead
2,3,4 of wands
cardinal fire

Taurus neck
5,6,7 of pentacles
fixed earth

Gemini shoulders
8,9,10 of swords
mutable air

Cancer chest
2,3,4 of cups
cardinal water

Leo solar plexus
5,6,7 of wands
fixed fire

Virgo colon
8,9,10 of
pentacles
mutable earth

Libra kidneys
2,3,4 of swords
cardinal air

Scorpio genitals
5,6,7 of cups
fixed water

Sagittarius thighs
8,9,10 of wands
mutable fire

Capricorn knees
2,3,4 of pentacles
cardinal earth

Aquarius ankles
5,6,7 of swords
fixed air

Pisces feet
8,9,10 of cups
mutable water

CHAKRA - ELEMENT
SUIT - COLOR

Crown Chakra
Major Arcana - XV-XXI
PURPLE

Third Eye Chakra
Major Arcana - VIII-XIV
INDIGO

Throat Chakra
Ether - Major Arcana I-VII
BLUE

Heart Chakra
Air - Swords
GREEN

Solar Plexus Chakra
Fire - Wands
YELLOW

Sexual Chakra
Water - Cups
ORANGE

Root Chakra
Earth - Pentacles
RED

This book is dedicated to Chris Crowhurst (1949–2020),
who was never afraid to create.

ACKNOWLEDGMENTS

I could not have done this book without the encouragement and help of Renee Bornstein; Laura Chatham; Mary Alice Fry; my twin brother, Marty Jacobs; May Kesler; Dehanna Rice; Terry Wolverton; and Michael.

I would also like to thank Helga A., Chris Crowhurst, Darci D'Anna, Jenny Holland, Brenda Hutchinson, Jennifer Jacobs, Roberta Mintz, Yvonne Owens, Genna Pinnick, Ali Schneider, Valerie Sonnenthal, Stephanie Swafford, and Anne Bridget Waters for their support.

I cannot forget the group who helped me at the brainstorming workshop with ideas for the "Suggested moves and props" portion of the card interpretations. Thank you April, Robin Dolan, Carolyn Gravely, Jennifer Jacobs, Akasha Madron, Val McHugh, and Tamara Starr.

Thanks also goes out to Carol Cannon, Grace Cloyd, Sandra Edwards, Louise Goeckel, and Robin Payne for their stories and quotes.

I am also grateful to the REDFeather team at Schiffer.

CONTENTS

Virtual Tarot in Motion

In 2020 the COVID-19 pandemic changed everything. Mandatory shutdowns caused live Tarot in Motion classes to be on hold for an unforeseeable amount of time. As a result, I began to teach classes virtually.

> Each year in late April, Dancer's Group[1] hosts Bay Area Dance Week,[2] a yearly dance festival that promotes free classes and performances. This year, due to the shutdowns, it was canceled.
> Dancer's Group suggested that instead of live classes, they'd offered to promote teachers' scheduled classes virtually. On a whim, I decided to go for it and offer a virtual Tarot in Motion. I chose to teach through Zoom, although other platforms may work just as well. I enjoyed teaching this way so much, I've continued offering virtual classes.

"Methods of Practicing Tarot in Motion" (chapter 1) can be followed as they are presented in this book, with some modifications. Here's what I discovered so far.

Virtual Tarot in Motion sessions can be offered to a broader audience who live other than locally.
Students are able to participate in the comfort of their own homes and still have cathartic experiences.
Instead of reviewing the structural guidelines (chapter 3) every time, email a file to participants ahead of time for review.
It's best to ask a basic question with or without seasonal emphasis for efficiency and to help unify the group. The card-reading portion has to be really quick, or I would lose everyone's attention.
I eventually skipped doing warm-up exercises or a meditation for virtual classes. An hour was enough time to hold a remote process-oriented class.
Break up larger groups into smaller ones or ask for volunteers to dance.

Pull a card from a deck for everyone or have participants pull cards from their personal decks or pull a card for them.
After pulling and having individual cards read, students may plan their dance by gathering props, costumes, and choice of music while others have their cards read. Encourage using their living space.
Follow steps for each presenting each dance.
Give time for presenting and processing dances.
Have some sort of closing, with end dancing together.

I think the online Tarot in Motion works so well because Miriam naturally holds the space for people in that unified field. Even though I'm in my own living room, I'm with other people. It seems very intimate.

I find that meaning that can be pulled from the cards and turned into movement is profound. I'm so much freer in my body. It's sacred work.

—*Darci*

For the computer screen:
Be aware of using the entire virtual space that shows up on your screen, whether it be close or farther away from the screen. Dance in your "box" screen. Reach low, high, diagonal, three-dimensional, head to toe.

From your pulled card, follow the Tarot in Motion structure chapter; choose no more than three attributes.
- body part = inner or outer definition of body part
- speed = slow, medium, fast
- movement quality = earth, water, fire, air, ether

1. Dancer's Group is a nonprofit organization that promotes the visibility and viability of dance in the San Francisco Bay Area. It is a hub for information, resources, writing on dance, free performances, and more. Check out https//:dancersgroup.org.
2. Bay Area Dance Week is a yearly ten-day festival that promotes free classes, workshops, and performances. It is one of the nation's largest, most inclusive celebrations of movement and dance.

> Dance speaks to us in every language.
> Dance is also a way to experience different aspects of our bodies on our own. It requires going beyond rational thinking.

Our body moves as our mind moves. The qualities of any movement are a manifestation of how mind is expressing through the body at that moment. Changes in movement qualities indicate that the mind has shifted focus in the body. So we find that movement can be a way to observe the expressions of the mind through the body, and it can also be a way to affect changes in the body-mind relationship.

—Bonnie Bainbridge Cohen[1]

PREFACE

The Dance of Miriam

Then the prophet Miriam, Moses' sister, took a tambourine in her hand, and all the women went out after her with tambourines and with dancing. And Miriam sang to them:

"Sing to the Lord, for he has triumphed gloriously; horse and rider he has thrown into the sea."[2]

My name, Miriam, means prophetess or rebellion.

In the Old Testament, Miriam was the revered sister and savior of her brother Moses, who later led the Hebrew people to flee Egypt. It's not always acknowledged that Miriam, along with her other brother, Aaron, had a big part in that procession as well.

In modern versions of the Passover story, it is believed that Miriam directed the women across the parted Red Sea with song and dance.

Could that dancing and singing have caused the sea to actually part?

When I dance a card, I always come away with a new understanding. The dancing allows me to relax into whatever is happening. A few years back while demonstrating a dance score, I asked the cards about the direction of Tarot in Motion. I pulled the Ace of Earth. I thought, "How can this be just the beginning?" At first, I was a little self-conscious. I had been facilitating Tarot in Motion for some time and was discouraged that I was only at the beginning.

The Ace of Earth indicates a new business adventure or planting a seed.

During my dance, I took a brown scarf and spiraled it into a tiny pile on the floor. I imagined that I was actually placing a seed into rich soil, all in front of the other participants. The Earth element reminds me to be patient. On a deeper level I understood the work's potential.

Many of us may have never thought of making up their own dance or a short theatrical piece to be witnessed, let alone from a Tarot card. There is something profound and healing that happens when Tarot in Motion dances are made.

-Miriam Jacobs

INTRODUCTION

How Tarot in Motion Came About

In order to heal, you need to change, and in order to change, you need to move.

In the 1980s, I was living in New York and making my way as a visual artist. In addition to creating my own work, I had the opportunity to absorb an amazing array of exhibitions and performances.

Merce Cunningham[3] choreographed the first nontraditional dance performance I ever saw. I decided to go because Robert Rauschenberg[4] had built the sets and John Cage[5] had provided the sound. I cannot say I really understood the Merce Cunningham concert, but it sparked an interest. I later learned that Cunningham and Cage pioneered the technique of not having the choreography coincide with the rhythms of the music. Instead they preferred to have the music and dance performed simultaneously yet independently of one another. Years later, I would play ambient music or sound in my Tarot in Motion sessions, likely inspired by the Cage and Cunningham collaboration.

During my time in New York, I also ran a not-for-profit poster-printing program at the Lower East Side Printshop[6], where I advised and instructed other not-for-profit groups to print their own advertising. Often I helped with posters for performance events, which raised my awareness of grassroots dance and theater events. The ones I was most drawn to weren't necessarily a particular style of dance but ones that had spiritually based content. I also loved when the performers showed passion more than technique.

Eventually the fumes from the printshop made me sick, and I had to leave that job. I started to explore alternative healthcare, including hands-on healing and herbs. I also began to study the Tarot and give readings for myself and others.

To say the least, I found those years challenging. Many people in my arts community were dying of AIDS. At one point, one of my colleagues asked me what I wanted to do. The answer was clear: I wanted to be a healer.

What drew me to Tarot was the quest to develop, affirm, and ground my growing intuition. It was really quite by accident that Tarot came into my life. My first deck was a gift. In all the upheavals going on in every aspect of my life, I wanted answers. I couldn't find reliance with anyone. Tarot became my teacher, and it still is.

My challenges at this time reminded me of my experiences as a child. I would have dreams both while sleeping and waking of going deep into my consciousness. In my dreams I imagined going to another dimension.

By the next fall, I was taking a training course in Polarity Therapy that emphasized making a body-mind connection. I noticed a similarity of the elements of Polarity to Tarot. Two years later as my training was concluding, I knew I was going to move to the Bay Area to open up a practice.

Several years into my practice, I started beginning many of my bodywork sessions with a brief Tarot card reading. The readings opened up conversations with my clients and set a direction for the session. It helped bring the client's unconscious layers to the surface and helped facilitate a deeper change.

In one particular instance, a client came to me very stressed out about the upheavals in her life. I had her pull four cards: three were very positive Major Arcana cards, and one was a very challenging Minor Arcana card. The reading calmed her down, which assured both of us that it was okay for her to change and gave me more possible bodily contacts to provide support.

Working in this way compelled me to create *Polarity Wellness Tarot* (*PWT*)[7], a body-based deck. Subsequently I wrote *Tarot and the Chakras: Opening New Dimensions to Healers (T&C).*[8]

PWT helped me improve my pre-session readings by showing the body connection for each card. *T&C* synthesized other systems to share with others.

After the deck and book, I thought that I wanted to teach Tarot in the context of yoga classes, but my love for dance won over. I began attending as many healing-arts dance classes as I could. Those classes exposed me to a wider perspective of the genre. I collaborated with a dancer friend and translated the symbols associated with the cards as a structure for creating healing dances.

I started holding my own Dancing the Tarot group sessions in 2014, which have evolved into being called Tarot in Motion.

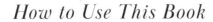

How to Use This Book

The handbook is organized in the following way:

- An explanation of the process of creating Tarot in Motion
- Guidelines for structuring Tarot in Motion
- A description of holiday rituals that can be incorporated into Tarot in Motion
- A description for each Tarot card
- Glossary-terminology

The Tarot in Motion handbook can be used for the following:

- A regular Tarot book with card meanings
- Group self-discovery sessions to create cathartic movement pieces
- Creating a dance in front of a mirror after pulling cards to help you learn Tarot in a new way
- For a one-on-one session in place of or addition to a hands-on bodywork session
- Inspiring content-rich choreography of performative dance

The handbook includes:

- A classic Tarot in Motion procedure
- Concise card interpretations without necessarily creating dances
- Guidelines to structure your dance or to just give you a place to begin
- Additional methods of practice; other session themes
- Tarot in Motion methods, with holiday rituals broken up into seasons
- Suggestions for longer workshops

WHAT IS TAROT IN MOTION?

Some people pull a card and the energy comes into their body.
Some are ready to get up and dance right away.
Some people don't quite know what to do and refer to the guidelines.

The whole is greater than the sum of its parts.

—Aristotle[9]

Tarot in Motion combines Tarot and movement in a playful way that is healing.

Restrictive problems on physical, mental, and emotional levels are more clearly seen and unwound. Tarot in Motion takes the message of the Tarot a step further than Tarot alone, by helping you get present and mindful in your body while embracing the awareness presented by the cards you have pulled.

There is something about pulling a card and having to create a movement piece that reaches past logic and taps into that wise inner knowledge hiding within yourself. The movement opens new perceptions. It's like magic.

The structure of your movement pieces are based on relating systems of your chosen cards, correlating to anatomical focal points based on Polarity Therapy, your chakras, qualities of related elements, movement pace, and, most importantly, the meaning of the card. This structure provides content rich guidelines for expressing what you have created.

The process is deceptively simple:
Have an intention, pull and interpret the card, then create a dance.

Have an intention:
Tarot in Motion dances requires an intention or a query. Intentions focus what is specifically being asked of pulled Tarot cards. Opened-ended questions are best because they empower you to personalize your own conclusions of the given interpretations.

Pull and interpret the card:
Interpret the pulled-card(s) meanings with the help of the descriptions of the cards, your own intuition, related symbols, and the illustrations.

What do other participants have to say? Does it resonate with you? What is the mood of the card? Let your movements be sparked by what you see and feel.

Create a dance:
When you are in front of a group of people, don't think; you just have to rely on muscle memory. You don't need to have prior dance or movement experience. Some of the most-beautiful pieces are created by participants who have never performed before. There is something raw and passionate that comes through. If you feel uncertain about the process, the "Guidelines" will help you get started.

Grace was really self-conscious about dancing in front of everybody. It took a lot of encouragement for her to come to class. By the end, Grace asked if there was any way she could have her dances videotaped the next time so she could see them.

You may write, draw your dance structure, just improvise, or someplace in between. Musical/sound options are available or chosen.

Dance in *Tarot in Motion* is used to mean any kind of intentional and purposeful movement; any type of dancing, theatrical acting, clowning, yoga, singing, or playfulness.

As a professional dancer choreographer, being present at live and virtual workshops over the past three years profoundly improved my craft. The group dynamic was open and nonjudgmental, yet the feedback was totally honest and helpful in generating fresh ideas for deeply personal performance pieces.

—*Mary Alice*

MY BRIEF SUMMARY OF DANCE HISTORY

Since the beginning of time, people have been dancing. Dance was once used for ceremonial and healing purposes as a part of everyday life. Integrated into each culture, dance now passes on the stories and history of a people.

Over time, dance evolved into a performative art form and became popular for social and recreational purposes.

By the twentieth century, modern dance revolutionized performative dance by no longer following strict rules and forms that often left a toll on dancers' bodies.

Out of modern dance came contemporary dance, which varied movement possibilities even more. Then came postmodern dance, which brought dancing back full circle to its healing origins.

The mother of postmodern dance is Anna Halprin,[10] an avant-garde Bay Area artist who recognized ordinary movement as dance. Anna brought dance into the community for expressing social causes. I once heard Anna say, "It becomes dance when you can feel it in your body."

Integrating dance with healing has become known to many as somatics, which means "of the body."

Somatics is also a term referred to in mind-body types of talk therapy and bodywork, where there is an awareness of changing the emotional and mental states through the body. A few illustrations of somatic bodywork are the Feldenkrais method, Rolfing, Hanna Somatics, and Polarity Therapy.

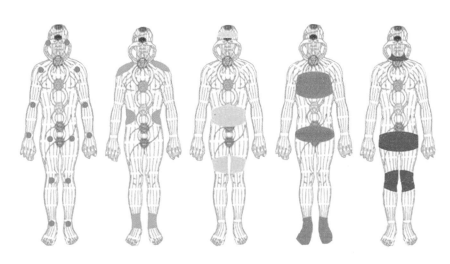

CHAPTER I

METHODS OF PRACTICING
TAROT IN MOTION

Laura has taken dance classes as a form of exercise her entire life. Until taking Tarot in Motion sessions, she never thought of performing. On a particular day, Laura pulled the Fool card, as a response to overcoming anxiety about her work as a teacher. The Fool encourages us to take risks and let go.

In her words, "After sharing my dance, the other participants reflected a dance back to me. I felt like I was understood."

Now, when Laura thinks of teaching, she feels supported. She realizes she just had to get out of her own way.

Laura goes on to say, "I'm always amazed that every time I pull a particular card, I think, 'Oh no, I'm never going to be able to dance this, and yet somehow from some place inside comes this idea that by the time I finish my dance, I really like what I did.'"

—*Laura*

This section explains the steps to use in every Tarot in Motion session, whether it is taking place in a group or done individually. Adapt these as you see fit.

If you are facilitating a group, it is polite to give credit to your sources and quotes whenever possible. At the same time, I encourage you to make the sessions and dances your own.

Tarot in Motion in a Group

Participants do not need to know one another beforehand.

A smaller group is between four and eight people. With fewer people, there is more intimacy and the facilitator can more easily manage the readings. Larger groups, more than eight people, may break up into pairs or smaller groups, preferably with at least one person who is familiar with Tarot in each group. Larger groups raise the level of excitement.

Environment: Select a large, empty space, studio, or gym, or outside on a flat field or the beach with audio capabilities such as speakers to hook-up jacks for iPhones, iPads, etc.

Be aware of your surroundings and any local or legal restrictions that may be enforced, such as sound restrictions and fire safety.

Time allowance: 1–3 hours

Clothing: Wear comfortable clothing to allow movement. Have participants wear layers if necessary. A variety of costumes and props may be provided. Participants can bring scarves, masks, and costumes that inspire them to share with others.

What to bring: Participants may bring personal Tarot decks, preferably the *Polarity Wellness Tarot*, yoga mats, blankets, writing and drawing materials, water bottles, and musical selections. Participants may be asked to bring personal altar objects.

Throughout every session include guided meditations, breath work, movement exercises, or free-form dancing.

> When Sharon first came to ongoing group sessions, she had never experienced Tarot before; she just wanted to move. By the end of the second session, she had already become adept at interpreting her own cards.

Preparation for a group session:

If the group is meeting for the first time, share previous experiences with both Tarot and dance. Provide a history for Tarot, and Tarot in Motion system and guidelines.

For every group session:

Establish clear time boundaries for beginning, steps, and ending times.
Find out if anyone has to leave early or knows if someone is going to be late.
Provide awareness of respecting the privacy of the session by not sharing with outsiders.
Give time for participants to ask questions.

Optional:
Clear the energy of the room by burning incense, candles, or a smudge stick involving participants or not. Ring bells and tap crystals while walking around the space. Call in the four directions.
Create an altar with meaningful items for that particular occasion: crystals, flowers, bells, fresh flowers, dried herbs, power objects, and anything fun. The facilitator can set this up, or the participants can take part and contribute objects as well.
Written exercises
Drawing or craft projects that relate to the theme
Offer gifts such as amulet bags, candles, or flower seeds that are significant to that particular occasion.
Have a closing ceremony to honor the end of the session by gathering in a circle, expressing gratitude and closing the four directions. This may be done by in a standing circle, holding hands, aloud, or in silence.
Allow time for socializing. Share snacks or a meal afterward.

General Procedure
You may choose to start and end with one or more of the above options.
Begin with free-form dancing and personal warm-ups, a quiet meditation, or a combination of these until all participants have arrived.
Gather in a standing circle with an introduction exercise, such as participants announcing their name accompanied by a simple but expressive motion. Have the other participants repeat the name and motion either individually or as a group. Larger groups may say each name in unison.
Give an explanation of the house rules (bathroom, breaks, etc.) and provide an outline of how the event will go.
Incorporate one or more guided movement exercises, meditation, or breath work during the session.
Regroup to a seated circle.
If you are facilitating or participating in a general Tarot in Motion session, think of a question or have an intention for pulling a Tarot card(s) from an individual or shared deck.
For holidays and celebrations, discuss the particular event and intention.
Help participants reframe questions for personalize inquiry (see p. 100).
Pull card(s) from an individual or shared deck.
Discuss card interpretations (in pairs or in a group), then select structures for developing a dance from the guidelines.
Offer the group time to plan the dance (10–20 minutes). Give everyone a set time to perform his or her own dance. *I find that two to three minutes is comfortable for newcomers.* Consider including costumes, props, music selections, and vocalizations.
A bell may be rung gently at the halfway point or a few moments before the dancer should end, iPhone timers work great.

Steps for presenting each dance:
Announce your card, so everyone knows you are beginning. Have individuals announce their card and any other introductions of their choice.
End with a bow or curtsy, so everyone knows (even you) that you've completed you dance. This sets a nonverbal boundary.
Witnesses clap.

In a group setting, viewers are referred to as "witnesses." Unlike in a performance setting, where an "audience" has the expectations of being entertained, "witnesses" are there to serve as a mirror for the transformations experienced by the dancer. However, it is also possible to practice Tarot in Motion by oneself in front of a mirror, where the dancer is her own witness.

Regroup and reflect:
Witnesses get to see the "aha" moment arise in a dancer (sometimes this happens hours or even days later). They witness you at your moment of vulnerability and realization. All judgment falls away. It's safe.
The witnesses are encouraged to give supportive feedback, not just on what they like about and why they like certain aspects of each other's dances, but how they thought it related to the pulled card and the query at hand. The witnesses are part of the process and are like mirrors reflecting back in words, affirming the meaning of the card. Of course the dancers also expressed what happened to them during the process, and respond to what the witnesses have shared.
The group size will determine how structured the reflection aspect of the session will be.

Gather for collective feedback, reflections, and support.
Encourage each performer to describe what they felt while being seen and what they noticed while witnessing others. What part did you like best?
Modify this to time boundaries and how much everyone participates.
Complete the session and socialize.

Tarot in Motion on Your Own

Benefits can still be gained from creating Tarot in Motion dances on your own.
Find a time when you will not be disturbed, and a space large enough to move freely.
Gather hats, scarves, robes, and masks to have on hand to possibly include in your dance.
Focus on an intention.
Ask your question and pull a card.
Write or draw in a journal before and after your dance.
Give yourself ten minutes or so to plan and prepare your dance.
While you are presenting your dance, pay particular attention to physical sensations and emotions that arise.
Consider dancing in front of a mirror or videotape yourself to watch later.

One-on-One Sessions

Tammy's clear intention for her one-on-one session was to overcome her fears of being alone. She knew it stemmed from spending the first few weeks of her life in an incubator. Yet, with all the work she had done around the issue, Tammy still hated to be alone.

After pulling a few cards, with my help, we created a makeshift incubator out of a few chairs, surrounded by some stiff mats placed upright, making what looked like a child's play fort.

Tammy climbed in, lying inside the "incubator." It took several tries and discussion until we found a position that was comfortable for me to gently pull her out. We then began to play like children.

A few days later, Tammy reported, "I got to experience the incubator I spent my first few weeks in, with someone there so I didn't feel so alone. It feels like part of the healing I'm doing around that wound."

A one-on-one session is set up as a private practitioner/client one-to-two-hour session. It will be planned on the needs of the client and will process a specific issue. The session will include a Tarot reading and planning out and creating a dance. *Sessions may include hands-on bodywork.*

The practitioner may dance with the client, be in conversation, or mirror moves. Other times the practitioner may just serve as a witness.

Gain more body awareness.
Change old patterns.
Come to sudden realizations.

"The process is deceptively
simple;... create a dance"

CHAPTER II

ADDITIONAL METHODS OF PRACTICE

Seeing myself dancing in the video afterwards was revelatory - had no idea this is the way I come across which dispelled some of my innate self-doubt and empowered me to better handle a difficult conversation scheduled for the next day.

—Carol

Here are some theme variations for a group Tarot in Motion session.

Personality & Soul Card Method[1]

Personality & soul cards give you some idea of who you are. It is a great way to get to know the Major Arcana cards. To find your personality and soul cards, draw only from the Major Arcana.

Personality cards show what you have come into this lifetime to learn, your outer expression and your talents.

Soul cards show your soul purpose, your deepest core, and individual expression.

Purpose: To learn about the personality and soul card(s) that represents you. Gain a better understanding of the Major Arcana.

Questions: Who are you? What qualities did you come into this lifetime with? What is your soul purpose?

Personality & Soul Card Formula

To determine your personality and soul card, add together the day, month, and year you were born.

If the sum is more than 22, add the single numbers together, resulting in the same card for both your personality and soul cards. If the sum is between 10 and 22, that number is your personality card. Add that number together to find your soul card.

Examples:

If your birthday is August 15, 1989, you would add up 8 + 15 + 1989 = 2012, then add 2 + 0 + 1 + 2 = 5. Since 5 is under 22, both your personality and soul cards are the Hierophant (5).

If your birthday is November 12, 1953, you would add up 11 + 12 + 1953 = 1976, then add 1 + 9 + 7 + 6 = 23, then add 2 + 3 = 5; both your personality and soul cards are the Hierophant (5).

If your birthday is May 3, 1975, you would add up 5 + 3 + 1975 = 1983, then add 1 + 9 + 8 + 3 = 21; your personality card is the World (21) and your soul card is the Empress (3).

Your birth date: _____

The number of the month I was born: _____

The date I was born: _____

The year I was born: _____

Add together: _____

Add each digit: ____+____+____+____ = _____

Double-digit answer: ____+_____ = _____

Personality number: (higher of the two numbers but less than 22) _____

Major Arcana card correspondence:_____

Soul number (single digit): _____ Major Arcana card correspondence: _____

These are the combinations of personality and soul cards:

Wheel of Fortune (10)	The Magician (1)
Justice (11)	The High Priestess (2)
The Hanged Man (12)	The Empress (3)
Death (13)	The Emperor (4)
Temperance (14)	The Hierophant (5)
The Devil (15)	The Lovers (6)
The Tower (16)	The Chariot (7)
The Star (17)	Strength (8)
The Moon (18)	The Hermit (9)
The Sun (19)	The Magician (1)
The Last Judgment (20)	The High Priestess (2)
The World (21)	The Empress (3)
The Fool (22)	The Emperor (4)

Year cards: If you want to find a card to guide you in the current year, you can use the same formula as above but replace your birth year with the current year.

Example: August 15, 2019, is 8 + 15 + 2019 = 2042, 2 + 0 + 4 + 2 = 8, then your personality and soul card for the year is Strength (8).

MOON DANCES

Pull cards and create dances both on the new and full moons, which both are powerful times due to the earth's energetic forces.
New moons are always in the sun sign they appear in.

Example: On April 23, 2020, the sun was in Taurus and the new moon was also in Taurus.

Full moons are always opposite the sun sign they appear in.

Example: On April 8, 2020, the sun was in Aries and the full moon was in Libra.

Explore by highlighting and asking questions to the traditional names of that month's full moon:

Example: In January, direct your question or intent to the wolf moon.

Traditional Full-Moon Names[2]

wolf moon	January
snow moon	February
worm moon	March
pink moon	April
flower moon	May
strawberry moon	June
buck moon	July
sturgeon moon	August
harvest moon	September or October
full corn moon (Harvest)	September
hunter's moon (Harvest)	October
beaver moon	November
cold moon	December

Explore using only the suit/element corresponding to the astrological sun, moon, and rising signs. Find out your sun, moon, and rising signs by consulting an astrologer.

ZODIAC	PHYSICAL FOCUS	CARDS/ELEMENT/SUIT[3]
Aries	forehead	2, 3, 4 of fire/wands
Taurus	neck	5, 6, 7 of earth/pentacles
Gemini	shoulders	8, 9, 10 of air/swords
Cancer	chest	2, 3, 4 of water/cups
Leo*	solar plexus	5, 6, 7 of fire/wands
Virgo	colon	8, 9, 10 of earth/pentacles
Libra	kidneys	2, 3, 4 of air/swords
Scorpio	genitals	5, 6, 7 of water/cups
Sagittarius	thighs	8, 9, 10 of fire/wands
Capricorn	knees	2, 3, 4 of earth/pentacles
Aquarius	ankles	5, 6, 7 of air/swords
Pisces	feet	8, 9, 10 of water/cups

Discovering the Element/Suits
Beforehand, go into extended details, discussing a particular suit and its related element. Have participants pull individual cards from that one suit. Then create solo and group scores.

Other possibilities: Divide participants into four smaller groups, each representing a different element/suit to form a dance.

Four Aces
Break the group up into four smaller groups. Create dances using only the four aces, with the intention of the seeds of that particular element.

Court Cards

Use only the sixteen court cards–this is particularly helpful for a team that works together. If there are more than sixteen participants, use court cards from two decks.

Questions: What is everyone's underlying role? How can individuals enhance their role for the best possible outcome?

Pull cards, discuss everyone's role, and then make an interactive group dance.

Anatomical Focusing

Facilitator leads a body scan meditation. See chapter XIII.

What part of your body did you most notice? Did you feel discomfort or pain? Or did you feel relaxed and opened?

Since body parts anatomically refer to three consecutive cards in the *Polarity Wellness Tarot*, which of those three cards do you relate the most to? Interpret and then dance that card.

Example: My shoulders ache. Shoulders correspond to 8, 9, and 10 of Air. So I can make a dance from one of these cards.

Birthday Dance

Figure out and discuss the birthday person's year card. See year card formula on p. 29.

Have all other guests pull cards, focusing on a message for the birthday person. Everyone dances their message for the birthday person, who is sitting in a chair in the middle of the room. Bend down to whisper in her ear a birthday blessing influenced by their pulled cards.[4]

Bridal Showers

Give the bride-to-be a four-to-ten-card Tarot reading. Have each of the other participants pull cards on how they can support the bride on her wedding or marriage.

Have the bride sit in the center. Take turns dancing to the bride, from the participants' individual pulled cards, using the formula on.

Include Visual Art and Drawing

Although it is getting away from moving and dancing, many movement-based expressive arts programs incorporate art making (and drawing) into healing-arts dancing. Incorporating visual arts may be another door of enlightenment.

Supply appropriate art materials such as drawing paper, crayons, colored pencils, markers, etc.

Here are a few occasions when you might incorporate visual art in your Tarot in Motion sessions:

On Valentine's Day, make Valentine cards for yourself.

On Easter, have an egg-dyeing party.

On Beltane, make garlands.

On the spring equinox, make a besom broom.

Spiritual, Emotional, Mental, and Physical Bodies

Draw or write about how you are feeling right now: spiritually, emotionally, mentally, and physically.

Shuffle and spread out your deck; pull four cards, laying them out from right to left and focusing on gaining insights to you: spiritually, emotionally, mentally, and physically, consecutively, to gain insights on what is happening on those levels. See the four-card spread in chapter XII.

Mask Making

Masks have been worn for centuries, for rituals and ceremonies to performances in all parts of the world. Something magical happens when we put on a mask. It gives us permission to be someone or something else. Incorporating masks can be very therapeutic.

Although mask making is an art unto itself, making masks out of paper plates opens something up in participants that would not have happened without being behind a mask.

Incorporate mask making within an open-ended Tarot in Motion session.

Supply art materials: Paper plates prepared with cutout holes for eyes and a way to tie or hold the mask up to the face. Drawing paper, crayons, colored pencils, markers, etc.

Musical choices: Participants choose from a genre or artistic band.

Example: After everyone asks a question and pulls a card, have them create a dance by using only Beatles songs.

Working with children: I suggest using an animal oracle deck, such as *The Wild Unknown Animal Spirit*[5] or *Medicine Cards*.[6] Or pick from the animals in Chinese astrology.[7]

Collaborations

Since we cannot all be experts in everything, invite someone to collaborate with.

Ask a breath-body-mind teacher, a specific dance form instructor, a mask maker, a meditation teacher, a shamanic drummer, or a yoga instructor.

CHAPTER III

GUIDELINES—STRUCTURED IMPROVISATION

I've explored different types of energy healing over the years, but what turned me on about this class is that on top of the mental and spiritual uplift, I was now creating movement that was cleansing and awakening. By my moving with intention, all of a sudden the healing awareness was translated into action, and I felt the shift immediately.

—Robin

TAROT IN MOTION CLASS BASIC OUTLINE

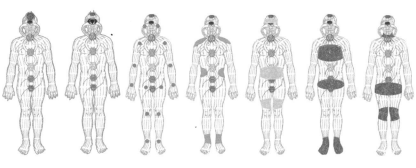

Major A	Major A	Major A	Swords	Wands	Cups	Pentacles
XV-XXI	VIII- XIV	I-VII	Heart/Air	Solar	Sexual/	Root/earth
Crown	Third eye	Throat/	shoulders	Plexus /Fire	Water	throat
		Ether	kidneys	3rd eye	chest	colon
			ankles	solar plexus	genitals	knees
		joints		thighs	feet	

ETHER/	AIR/SWORDS	FIRE/WANDS	WATER/CUPS	EARTH/
MAJORS	LIGHT	STRONG	FLOWING	**PENTACLES**
EXPANSIVE	SCATTERED	SHAKING	SMOOTH	GROUNDED
ELONGATED	AGILE	ASSERTIVE	CONNECTING	STEADY
STILL	*dance*	*visual arts*	*cooking*	SLOW
music	**YAM**	**RAM**	**VAM**	*sculpture*
HAM				**LAM**

 Quick

 Slow

 Moderate

> The reason the guidelines are powerful is because they relate to the cards; there is meaning behind them.

Guidelines are your structural-resource options associated with every card to generate movement material. They help you gain a visceral understand of the cards.

The guidelines provide the fine line between having a structure and improvising. Having a structure focuses your mind from distraction. They help you express the meaning of the card(s) so others will comprehend your dance.

Improvising is spontaneous and brings the unconscious to the surface. Twyla Tharp[1] says, "There's a fine line between good planning and overplanning. You never want the planning to inhibit the natural evolution of your work."[2]

Guideline suggestions are in every card description. The symbols for the guidelines appear in a sequential strip on top of every card description and on each *PWT* card.

Symbols occur in many cultures as a way to communicate with each other.

A symbol strip appears like this:

Resource for guidelines: Use as many or few as you like.
The Card Meaning
Expressive-Movement Qualities
Pace
Chakra
Anatomical Focus
Astrological-Sign References

Other Options to choose include these:
Music, sounds, and vocalizations
Pathway possibilities

The Card Meaning

Look up the written Tarot card meaning of your pulled card(s). Consider your prior knowledge. How does the card relate to what you know? Look up the related elements, physical focus, and astrological correspondences. What does the card mean to you on the basis of your intuition? How does it apply to the specific question?

Ask open-ended questions such as these:

How can I best approach the *situation*?
How do I balance _____?
How do I best overcome the challenge?
What are the implications of my choices?
What is going on?

Expressive-movement qualities: Expressive-movement qualities are determined by the elements that relate to the suits of Tarot. The elements prompt essential properties to express your dance.

Element		Suit[3]
⧖	Ether	Major Arcana
△	Air	Swords
△	Fire	Wands
▽	Water	Cups
▽	Earth	Pentacles

A secondary or sub-element is from the element that the astrological sign references for a particular card.

Example: The 9 of Water/Cups has Jupiter in Scorpio.

Elemental-movement qualities: Water (Scorpio) with earth (Jupiter)
Water is the main element and earth is the secondary element or subelement.
Use either the main or secondary element for your dance:

The ether element: Accepting, acknowledging, centered, elongated, expansive, grief, jealous, listening, open, proud, silent, spiritual, sound, or spacey

The air element: Bargaining, brilliant, caring, charitable, compassionate, considering, desirous, empathetic, envious, examining, fast, giddy, high strung, jittery, joyful, jumpy, talkative, laughing, judging, or quick witted

The fire element: Active, angry, bright, controlling, creative, charismatic, dominant, enthusiast, forgiving, frustrating, persuasive, potent, powerful, resentful, shaking, thrilled, vital, or willful

The water element: Accepting, addictive, belonging, bonding, boundary less, compulsive, connecting, emotional, flowing, fluid, kind, loving, nurturing, overbearing, sensual, sensitive, sexy, or smooth

The earth element: Contracted, courageous, fearful, greedy, grounded, insecure, lazy, organized, practical, secure, solid, steady, slow, strong, or stubborn

Pace

Although your dance may combine various paces, I've calculated one of three basic paces for every Tarot card to (at least) begin your dance with: quick, moderate, slow/still.

The quick is shown with **(+)**, the moderate with **(-)**, and the slow/still with **(o).**

Changing the awareness of the speed of movement may also bring physical, mental, or emotional changes, bringing the unconscious to the surface.

Paces are derived from the three principles of touch in Polarity Therapy that also synchronize with the astrological modes: cardinal, fixed, and mutable signs. See chapter IV.

Major Arcana Card Paces

The Major Arcana pace suggestions are determined by their associated astrological or planetary signs.

Minor Arcana Card Paces

(o) All aces represent the pure essence of the suit and element. Choosing an ace suggests using a slow or neutral pace.

⊕ All the 2s, 3s, and 4s suggest beginning your dance with a quick pace.
Ọ All the 5s, 6s, and 7s suggest beginning your dance with a slow or almost still pace.
⊖ All the 8s, 9s, and 10s suggest beginning your dance with a moderate pace.

Court Card Paces come from their patriarchal rank:

(+)	King	Father / wise one	Air	quick
(−)	Queen	Mother/nurturer	Water	moderate
(+)	Knight	Son / young adult	Fire	quick
(o)	Page	Daughter/child	Earth	slow

Chakras

Chakras are the seven basic energy centers that line up along our spines, bridging the body to consciousness, ourselves to the world. Relating the chakras to their original Vedic elemental names and then to the Tarot suit of your pulled card gives you another possibility to structure your dance.

Undulating (moving like waves) from a specific chakra may activate that chakra's particular vibration.

Physical Focus

A physical focus grounds and exemplifies the meaning of a Tarot card, bringing it into your body, especially if it already relates to your pulled card. The body part to accentuate appears under each card description in *Tarot in Motion*. They also appear in colored highlights in the "Polarity Man" on each *PWT* card. The aces and court cards represent all three anatomical references for every suit.

Astrological-Sign References

Incorporate anything you know about the card's related astrological and planetary symbols into your dance. Think about people in your life who are born under those particular signs. Or find the "astrologic influence" under each card description.

The astrological information given sometimes opposes the card meaning. Use what works for you.

Then, the music shifted. I stopped and threw my head back and the purple beads on my head went crashing to the floor. It was as if I had thrown off a great load.

—Laura

Music and Sound

I recommend choosing ambient music or vibrational-sound music in the background so people won't tend to dance just to the music. The music helps contain the space, although sometimes a certain musical piece is appropriate.

Create a musical playlist to dance for the beginning and ending of Tarot in Motion sessions and for including particular meditations, for instance.

Other Inspirations

Pathway Possibilities

Circular, zigzag, back and forth, in one place (star, square, spiral)—what comes to your mind? Most participants do not consciously choose a pathway. Does changing a pathway shift something in you?

Here are some structural possibilities:

Major Arcana	dance in a spiral
Air/Swords	dance in a star
Fire/Wands	dance in a triangle
Water/Cups	dance in a circle
Earth/Pentacles	dance in square

Card Numbers

The number of the card may possibly be utilized in a number of ways:
Steps in a sequence
Number of participants in a group dance

CHAPTER IV

ADDITIONAL INFORMATION FOR GUIDELINES

The elements referred to in *Tarot in Motion* are based on the four active elements found in nature, plus a fifth element, ether, which is the container of the four active

ETHER:	AIR	FIRE	WATER	EARTH
ASTROLOGICAL: The entire body	ASTROLOGICAL: Gemini shoulders Libra kidneys Aquarius ankles	ASTROLOGICAL: Aries forehead/eyes Leo solar plexus Sagittarius thighs	ASTROLOGICAL: Cancer breasts Scorpio pelvis Pisces feet	ASTROLOGICAL: Taurus neck Virgo colon Capricorn knees
COLOR: blue ART: music CHAKRA: throat sense of hearing	COLOR: green ART: dance CHAKRA: heart sense of touch	COLOR: yellow ART: visual arts CHAKRA: solar plexus sense of sight	COLOR: Orange ART: cooking CHAKRA: sexual sense of taste	COLOR: red ART: sculpture CHAKRA: root Sense of taste
MENTAL BODY: Open, connected to spirit	MENTAL BODY: analyzing, witty, clear	MENTAL BODY: focus, clear, upfront	MENTAL BODY: inclusive understanding intuitive	MENTAL BODY: practical patient structured
EMOTIONAL BODY: Grief/return to spirit	EMOTIONAL BODY: compassion/desire	EMOTIONAL BODY: forgiveness/ enthusiasm anger, resentment	EMOTIONAL BODY: letting go/ attachment	EMOTIONAL BODY: courage/fear
PHYSICAL BODY: throat joints cranial sacral system thyroid gland ears	PHYSICAL BODY: lungs and chest nervous system skin thymus gland	PHYSICAL BODY: solar plexus digestive system liver, gallbladder pancreas	PHYSICAL BODY: generative organs menstrual cycle lymphatic systems secretion glands	PHYSICAL BODY: bones colon muscles
TISSUE QUALITY: elongated	TISSUE QUALITY: movement and speed nerve reflexes	TISSUE QUALITY: shaking (heat)	TISSUE QUALITY: smooth, flowing	TISSUE QUALITY: contraction strong tone
VOICE QUALITY: open flaccid self-expressive	VOICE QUALITY: fast, jumpy, scattered	VOICE QUALITY: loud, sharp, clear, staccato	VOICE QUALITY: rhythmic flowing calm	VOICE QUALITY: slow deep steady
SEED MANTRA: HAM GEMSTONE: moonstone SEASON: All DIRECTION: All	SEED MANTRA: YAM GEMSTONE: emerald SEASON: Spring DIRECTION: East	SEED MANTRA: RAM GEMSTONE: coral SEASON: Summer DIRECTION: South	SEED MANTRA: VAM GEMSTONE: pearl SEASON: Autumn DIRECTION: West	SEED MANTRA: LAM GEMSTONE: ruby SEASON: Winter DIRECTION: North

This chart is complied from a several of Polarity Therapy sources.

Elements

The elements referred to in *Tarot in Motion* are based on the four active elements found in nature, plus a fifth element, ether, which is the container of the four active elements.

Paces

In dance and music, pace is referred to as tempo.

The tempo is the speed or pace of a given dance or musical composition. Technically speaking, tempo is measured by beats per minute (bpm).

Since every planet exalts an astrological sign, all Major Arcana cards have a referential mode, and therefore each suggests a pace. "Exalts" in this context refers to the placement of a planet in a particular sign where the planet is in its highest power.

The paces are borrowed and then translated from the three Polarity principles (rajas, tamas, and sattvas). They also are derived from the three astrological modes, known as cardinal, fixed, or mutable, which have a correspondence to every Tarot card.

Symbols for astrological modes (seasonal alignments) suggest the pace for your piece.

The beginning of a season, cardinal signs suggest a rapid **(+)** tempo

The middle of a season, fixed signs suggest a slow **(o)** tempo.

The end of a season, mutable signs suggest a moderate **(−)** tempo.

Astrological signs fall either in the beginning, middle, or end of one of the four seasons (spring, summer, fall, and winter). These are known as astrological modes. The three modes (cardinal, fixed, and mutable) have certain aspects differentiating them from each other.

They also correspond to the three principles (and three types of touch) in Polarity Therapy and the three gunas in Ayurveda.

Cardinal signs are the signs at the beginning of a season: Aries, Cancer, Libra, and Capricorn. Cardinal signs are always the 2, 3, and 4 cards and suggest a quick pace.

People born under a cardinal sign are instigators, energetic, fast, initiators, and leaders. They are active, self-motivated, insightful, and ambitious. Cardinal signs are sometimes called reactive signs.

Fixed signs are the signs in the middle of a season: Taurus, Leo, Scorpio, and Aquarius. Fixed signs are always the 5, 6, and 7 cards and suggest a slow or almost still pace.

People born under a fixed sign are stable, determined, and persistent. They are stable, strong, and stubborn. At times they can also be inflexible, stubborn, opinionated, and single-minded.

Mutable signs are at the end of a season: Gemini, Virgo, Sagittarius, and Pisces. Mutable signs are always the 8, 9, and 10 cards and suggest a moderate pace.

People born under a mutable sign are adaptable and changeable. They tend to mediate change and vary their modes of expression frequently in order to meet this end. They are often described as being diplomatic and assist others through transitions.

Chakras

Lining up chakras is a popular tool for meditation. The two upper chakras bridge your spirit to the universal spirit. The five lower chakras bridge your spirit to the body. Each chakra has a Sanskrit name, symbol, color, sound vibration, and purpose.

For more on the chakras, see *Tarot and the Chakras: Opening New Dimensions to Healers*.

Element	Chakra	Tarot Suit	Statement	Sanskrit name
	Crown	Major Arcana XV–XXI	I understand	*Shasrara*
	Eye	Major Arcana VIII–XIV	I see	*Ajna*
	Throat	Major Arcana 0–VII	I speak	*Vishuddha*
	Heart	Swords	I love	*Anahata*
	Solar Plexus	Wands	I do	*Manipura*
	Sexual	Cups	I feel	*Swadistana*
	Root	Pentacles	I am	*Muladhara*

Crown Chakra ("I understand")
Located at the top of the head, the crown chakra is the point where energy flows into the entire chakra system from cosmic source. The crown chakra has the lightest, finest, and highest-frequency vibration. This chakra is about being present and truly letting go. It contributes to healing and feeling whole. The crown chakra is associated with the color purple and the planet Uranus, which frees us from limitations.

Third-Eye Chakra ("I see")
Located in the middle of the forehead, the third eye is about inner vision. It correlates to the planet Jupiter, which emphasizes truth. The third-eye chakra is where psychic abilities are experienced, enabling one to see as if with a "third eye." It is known as the seat of wisdom and is associated with the deep-blue color indigo.

Ether (Throat) Chakra ("I speak")
Located in the middle of the throat, the ether chakra is the place that connects our spiritual body to our physical body. It is about finding our own voice and how to communicate that voice to others. The ether chakra is vibration, sound, and space. Like the ether element, it is associated with the color blue. The planet representation is Mercury, which further emphasizes communication.

Air (Heart) Chakra ("I love")

Not surprisingly, the air chakra is in the middle of the chest, behind the heart, and is all about self-acceptance, compassion, and desire. The air chakra is about well-being, peace, and connection. Green is the color association, and the planet is Venus, which brings us love.

The air chakra is the midway point between all seven chakras and helps us separate and then integrate.

Fire (Solar Plexus) Chakra ("I do")

Located right above the navel, the fire chakra influences our self-esteem, passion, and will. The fire chakra governs our ego, both positively and negatively. The planetary association of Mars gives it drive and courage. It is a very male energy. The color yellow is associated with this chakra. It supplies us with heat radiating from the sun. This chakra is a good place to imagine letting energy out of.

Water (Sacral/Sexual) Chakra ("I feel")

Located in the lower abdomen and the reproductive organs, the water chakra is about flow and often sexuality. It is about making and keeping connections of all kinds. It provides an emotional basis and gives us a sense of ourselves. Orange is the color associated with this chakra. Its planet is the moon, whose influence is adaptable and reflective. The water chakra is female power based.

Earth (Root) Chakra ("I am")

Located at the base of our spine and our pelvic floor, the earth chakra grounds us. It gives us support in physical, emotional, and spiritual ways. The earth chakra gives us a feeling of belonging and touches our instinctual needs. It influences literal factors in our lives, such as money, career, and our physical bodies. The color association of the earth chakra is red, and its planetary influence is Saturn, which supplies order and form. It is where kundalini energy rises.

For a more extensive description of the chakras, also see the book *Tarot and the Chakras*.

Astrological	Zones of the Body
Aries	forehead
Taurus	neck
Gemini	shoulders
Cancer	chest
Leo	solar plexus
Virgo	colon
Libra	kidneys
Scorpio	genitals
Sagittarius	thighs
Capricorn	knees
Aquarius	ankles
Pisces	feet

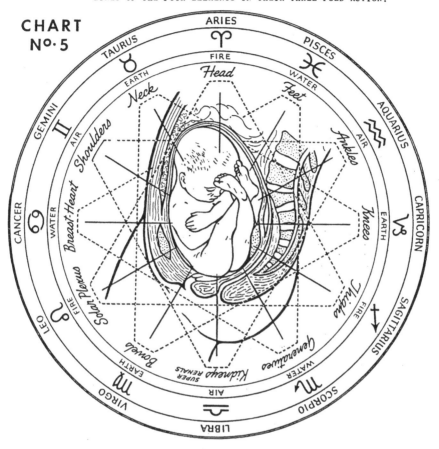

CHART Nº·5

The position of the child in the mother's womb is the natural squatting posture of man, where all energy currents can flow freely to produce a perfect human body, and for maintaining good health after birth and throughout life in this world. (Please refer to my book, "EASY STRETCHING POSTURES FOR VITALITY AND BEAUTY". This is the origin of it and here is the reason for its fine results as a NATURAL HEALTH EXERCISE.)

The body reference points of Tarot in Motion are from this popular Polarity Therapy chart.1

From Polarity Therapy, Book II: The Wireless Anatomy of Man, Chart 5, Randolph Stone

Astrology

Here are some basic astrological meanings.

Aries: cardinal fire—focused on new experiences, active and outgoing, assertive, self-willed, starting things off, and new beginnings. The RAM.

Taurus: fixed earth—secure, stubborn, slow, possessive, strong, loving comfort and beauty, possessions and comforts. The BULL.

Gemini: mutable air—quick, light, talkative, indecisive, adaptable, perceptive and friendly, duality. The TWINS.

Cancer: cardinal water—compassionate, sensitive, nurturing, protective, and connecting mother to child. The CRAB.

Leo: fixed fire—bright, proud, dramatic, adventurous, charging ahead, and creative. The LION.

Virgo: mutable earth—meticulous, orderly, service, order and control, and detail oriented. The VIRGIN.

Libra: cardinal air—balanced, just, harmonious balance, and truth. The SCALES.

Scorpio: fixed water—passionate, deep, fearless, fixed sign, merging through sexuality, and the occult. The SCORPION.

Sagittarius: mutable fire—big-hearted, idealistic, restless, focused on a target, and "out there" energy. The ARCHER.

Capricorn: cardinal earth—solid, cautious, structured, self-controlled, taking care of earthly needs, and career. The GOAT.

Aquarius: fixed air—trendsetter, extremist, individualistic individuals, and rulers. The WATER CARRIER.

Pisces: mutable water—romantic, idealistic, compassionate, merging with spirituality, and letting go of karma. The FISH. [2]

Planets

☉	Sun	ego identity, radiant spirit, individuality	fire
☾	Moon	emotions, adaptable sense of self, reflective	water
☿	Mercury	reason, skill, intelligence, verbal expression	air
♂	Venus	love, attraction, compassion, connection	earth
☿	Mars	drive, desire, courage	fire
♃	Saturn	order, form, disciplined, fear, contraction, transcendence	fire
♄	Jupiter	truth, faith, grace, optimistic, expansive	earth
♅	Uranus	free from limitations, willful, inventive, rebellious	water
♆	Neptune	formless, escapist, spiritual realized	water
♇	Pluto	transformative, regenerative, subversive	air

CHAPTER V

TAROT IN MOTION WITH HOLIDAYS

Our experiences are gently nudged into a different context by reframing our card questions. As we take in the hints the cards offer, and integrate them into our scenarios, our bodies and art start to express different angles to our own stories—from within.

In an almost magical way, the group reflects, amplifies, and supports each other's experiences.

—Helga

On specific days of the year, you may want to commemorate a holiday of cultural or religious significance. Incorporating Tarot in Motion encourages us to deepen the significance of that celebration.

Tarots in Motion holiday events are broken up into the four seasonal sections: spring, summer, autumn, and winter. Each section includes a solar event, a midpoint event, and other holidays that occur within that season.

Having a theme and basic question for a Tarot in Motion session fosters group connection. While still keeping the meaning of the celebration in mind, I encourage you to come up with modified rituals, intentions, and unifying questions. The purpose and questions may pose mere suggestions.

The Eight Seasonal Celebrations

"The Witch's Wheel" is the eight-spoked wheel of the seasonal year. Wiccan and ancient Eurocentric traditions observe eight major sacred festivals evenly spaced around the yearly cycle.

These midpoints are marked by solar and astral celestial events and served as seasonal signposts for ancient agrarian societies. They were used to determine the correct times for planting; harvesting, winnowing, and fallowing periods were gauged by this very accurate system of solar/lunar/astral timekeeping.

The four solar events:
Winter solstice or Yule
Spring equinox
Summer solstice
Autumn equinox

The four midpoints events:
Samhain ("Sow'-en")
Imbolc ("Im'-olg")
Beltaine ("Bel'-chin-uh")
Lammas ("Lamma") or Lughnasa ("Loo na-sah")[1]

Each celebration description provides the following:
Background: A basic historical description of the celebration, with personal tidbits
Intention: A focused purpose with a reference to the celebration
Question(s) to ask: Suggested related question(s) to focus on while shuffling, spreading out, and pulling cards from an individual or shared deck
Special materials to bring: Are always optional. Although materials may be provided, a facilitator may ask participants to bring specific items to enhance and personalize the session.
Other possibilities: Are always optional. They may include other related activities or altar objects to include in the session.

Winter

WINTER SOLSTICE (YULE)
December 20–22 (precise date varies year to year)
Inspired by Anne Bridget Waters[2]

Background: The winter solstice, the first day of winter, is the moment the North Pole is tilted farthest away from the sun, making it the shortest day and the longest night of the year. Also known as Yule, the winter solstice is the conception point of the year.

Winter is a great time for staying warm and telling stories, so we add storytelling inspired by the Tarot cards we have pulled for our dances.

"Everybody has a story. In learning, we tend to remember stories better than direct information. Stories bring complex ideas to everyday understanding."

Intention: To feel comfortable with the onset of winter. Learn how to include your voice with dances.

Question(s) to ask: What card can help me tell my story?
Tell stories combining dancing inspired by your pulled cards.

Special materials to bring: A journal and your favorite pen. Warm blankets and shawls.

Other possibilities: Continue the thread of a story; when there is a pause (or set time), the next person continues a story based on their card.
Incorporate adjacent holidays such as Christmas, Hanukkah, Kwanzaa, etc.
Exchange gifts.
Include an altar decorated with stringed Christmas lights, and evergreens. Offer candles to signify the bringing back of the light. Share a meal or snacks.

NEW YEAR
January 1

Background: There are dozens of activities or rituals to choose from to bring in the New Year, from partying all night, ringing in the New Year with horns and whistles, and a champagne toast to serving a special meal. Some people go on meditation retreats, while others build a bonfire or even take a plunge in the ocean.

There is always an energy buildup that can be felt on New Year's, however you choose to participate. Treat whatever you do as a ritual to bring in a big change.

Intention: To give New Year spiritual meaning. Announce and then embrace your outward resolutions and internal intentions.

Question(s) to ask: What are my goals for the next year? How do I best attain and maintain my New Year's resolutions and intentions? What do I want to bring into the New Year? What should I leave behind?

Special materials to bring: Noise makers, bells, horns, and confetti

Other possibilities: Eat black-eyed peas with cornbread, symbolizing good luck and prosperity. Make a toast with a bubbly beverage. Offer empty amulet bags to be filled at home.

IMBOLC
February 1–2
Inspired by Marcela Lobos, the rite of the womb[3]

Background: Imbolc is the halfway mark between the winter solstice and the spring equinox. It is the festival of the "maiden" part of the year, where seeds of spring begin to stir. The celebration of Imbolc dates back to the pre-Christian era in the British Isles.

Early Christians knew Imbolc as St. Brigit's Day, for the saint associated with fertility. It was also called Candlemas, from fourth-century Greece, when candles were lit to symbolize of the return of light and a time of purification.

Ground Hog Day is the modern version of Imbolc.

Imbolc is a time to connect to our fertility and to our wombs. I am inspired to bring the ritual of the thirteenth rite into this session.

Take turns having each woman facing the woman next to her (men can do this too). Begin by placing your own hands on your own heart and womb. Transmit the wisdom from your womb to hers by saying the below quote individually or in unison.

Next, place your hands on her womb and then take her hands, placing them on her own womb. She affirms that she received the wisdom in her womb and repeats the process with the woman next to her.

Repeat or paraphrase this:

"Let's heal our womb; the womb is not a place to store fear and pain; the womb is to create and give birth to life. Let's heal our mother's, sister's, and daughter's wombs. And in this way bring healing to our Mother Earth."

—Marcela Lobos

Intention: To connect to our wombs and bring healing to Mother Earth

Question(s) to ask: How do I best empower myself and other women?

Special materials to bring: Show the video of the thirteenth rite on the website. Or tell the background story.

Other possibilities: Include an altar of flowers and crystals with photos of you as a young child, or being pregnant. Include playfulness in your dances to represent the maiden within. Tell your own womb stories. Offer smudge sticks. Have snacks of milk products such as cheese and seeds.

VALENTINE'S DAY
February 14

Background: Valentine's Day is based on commemorating Saint Valentine, a Roman priest of the third century who was beheaded for performing wedding ceremonies at a time when there was a military ban on marriages. Other roots are from a pagan matchmaking festival called Lupercalia.

I'd like to start the trend of making Valentine's Day a reminder to love ourselves. In order to find love, you have to first love yourself.

Intention: Learn to love yourself more than you imagined.

Question(s) to ask: How can I deepen my love for myself? How do I best expand my relationship with_____? How do I open my heart? How can I love my body, my work, my home more?

Special materials to bring: Roses, red and pink ribbons, rose quartz crystals, and symbols of hearts. Bring a close friend.

Other possibilities: Set up an altar with the above materials. Offer Valentine's cards to write to yourself. Chant "I love myself with all my heart" until it becomes a song.

Spring

SPRING/VERNAL EQUINOX (OSTARA)
Occurs between March 20 and 23 (precise time varies year to year)

Background: The spring/vernal equinox is better known as the first day of spring. It is a popular time to do a major house cleaning and metaphorically a time of letting go.

Intention: To sweep away the old with a symbolic broom of what no longer serves you, making room for abundance and joy

Question(s) to ask: What and how do I need to clean up?

Special materials to bring: A feather or a symbolic broom

Other possibilities: Include an egg-balancing ceremony on the exact time of the equinox. Provide enough raw chicken eggs for each participant to try to stand one or two eggs on their ends. Then cook and eat your eggs. Offer packets of flowering seeds.

In ancient Chinese and in modern-day pagan traditions, it is considered good luck to balance eggs. It is important to do this ritual at the exact moment of the equinox, because that is when the universe is most balanced.

While still living in New York City, I met Mama Donna Henes,[5] the Urban Shaman, who introduced me to doing seasonal ceremonies. My favorite was for the vernal equinox, when eggs could be balanced on their ends. For the past forty-five years, Mama Donna has gotten hundreds of people to balance eggs on their ends at public events throughout the city.[6]

APRIL FOOLS DAY
April 1

Background: The origins of April Fools Day, April 1, began with Pope Gregory XIII, who in 1582 wanted his new Gregorian calendar to replace the old Julian calendar. This called for a New Year's Day to be celebrated on January 1 instead of the end of March. But some people apparently didn't get the memo and continued to celebrate New Year's Day on April 1. These poor folk were made fun of and were sent on "fools errands" for a laugh.

April Fool's Day could also have been a holiday celebrated the end of winter.

April Fool's Day is typically a day to play practical jokes and pranks, especially for children.

In the Tarot, the Fool is the beginning of Major Arcana cards, represent by 0. Both the Fool card and April Fools Day correspond to the astrological sign Aries. Both represent (another) new beginning.

Intention: Enjoy being foolish.

Question(s) to ask: What risks shall I take at this moment? What can I do on a whim? What do I need to laugh at within myself?

Special materials to bring: Practical jokes

Other possibilities: After dancing individual dances, end with a group dance of silly dancing.

PASSOVER
Begins in March or April (on the fifteenth day of the month of Nisan in the Jewish calendar)

Background: Also called Pesach, the eight-day Jewish festival celebrates in commemoration of the passing over or freeing from slavery of the Israelites in Egypt.

Passover begins with one or two evenings of a religious ceremonial Seder, a ritualistic meal to remind us of our freedom by retelling story the Passover story.

Feminist sources believe that it was Miriam, the sister of Moses, and a Hebrew goddess, who led the women and children out of Egypt by dancing, song, and drums through the parting of the Red Sea. The pagan roots of Passover are from a springtime purification rite honoring Miriam.

Intention: Understanding the history of Passover. Celebrating what freedom means.

Question(s) to ask: What does my freedom look like? How can I change course?

Special materials to bring: Items that personally represent freedom to you. Drums, bells, and rattles.

Other possibilities: Include an altar of a Seder plate. Take turns leading dances in a circle or a spiral. Offer pieces of matzos, the significant unleavened bread of Passover.

EASTER
Usually held in April, on the first Sunday after the full moon after the equinox

Background: Easter is a Christian holiday that celebrates the resurrection of Jesus Christ.
Easter was also when eggs could finally be eaten after Lent, a forty-day cleansing period. Eggs symbolized the resurrection as well as new life.
The word "Easter" is derived from the Greek and Latin *pasch*, for Passover. It is quite possible that the last supper was a Passover Seder.
Early Christians painting eggshells red represented the blood of Jesus. Greeks, Ukrainians, and predynastic Egyptians all included customs of painting eggs.
Easter egg hunts and egg rolling are two popular egg-related traditions. An egg hunt involves hiding eggs outside for children to run around and find on Easter morning. Eggs are rolled as a symbolic reenactment of the rolling away of the stone from Christ's tomb.

Intention: Ritualizing Easter. Understanding the history of Easter.

Question(s) to ask: What do I need to resurrect?

Special materials to bring: Colored hardboiled eggs

Other possibilities: Wear or make Easter bonnets. Include an altar with dyed hardboiled eggs and tulips. Instead of hiding eggs, hide Tarot cards! Read and make Tarot in Motion dances out of the cards you find. Offer tiny marbled eggs.

BELTANE
May 1

Background: Beltane marks the (relative) halfway point between the spring equinox and the summer solstice. Beltane means "bright light" or "lucky fire." This is when spring is in full bloom, a festivity of youth, mating, and fertility.

Beltane celebrates the profound blessings of spring and the coming abundance of summer. To celebrate, people made garlands and danced around bonfires.

Beltane has evolved into May Day, which, although celebrated slightly differently in various places, still holds traces of Beltane. The dancing is often circled around a maypole. In socialist countries, May Day has become known as International Workers' Day.

Intention: To build community, and to purify and celebrate our youth

Question(s) to ask: Ask your younger self: What can I offer you in order to heal?

Special materials to bring: Flowers; floral-printed clothing to wear.

Other possibilities: Include an altar with a basket of spring flowers. Perform dances outside in a flat field around a tree or pole to represent a maypole. Create an actual maypole. Make garlands or floral crowns. Bring something reminiscent of your teens. Play games. Offer flowers.

MOTHER'S DAY
The second Sunday in May

Background: Mother's Day recognizes mothers, motherhood, and maternal bonds in general. It was started by Anna Jarvis in 1908 at St. Andrew's Methodist Church in Grafton, West Virginia.

Intention: Loving our mothers

Question(s) to ask: How do I best nurture myself? And nurture others?

Special materials to bring: A photo of your mother and other women who influenced your upbringing

Other possibilities: Include an altar with roses and items representing your mother. Choose dancing from the following Tarot cards:
• The Empress is the grounded, nurturing mother figure.
• The Queen of Air is focused.
• The Queen of Fire is passionate.
• The Queen of Water loves.
• The Queen of Earth is practical.
Take turns being guided by each of the queens.

FATHER'S DAY
The third Sunday in June

Background: Father's Day honors fathers and celebrates fatherhood, paternal bonds, and the influence of fathers in society. It is similar to Mother's Day but has older ties. Father's Day is connected to St. Joseph's Day (early 1500s). There were several attempts to establish it as a holiday, including in 1911 by Jane Addams, an American Settlement activist, and in 1915 by Lions Club member Harry C. Meek.

Intention: To examine what do our fathers mean to us, and how to appreciate them
Question(s) to ask: What has my father taught me? How can I resolve my "father issues"?

Special materials to bring: A photo of your father and father figures in your life

Other possibilities: Include an altar representing your father. Choose dancing from the following Tarot cards:
The Emperor is a kind, benevolent leader.
The King of Air is objective.
The King of Fire is confident.
The King of Water is benevolent.
The King of Earth is authoritative and stable.
Take turns being guided by each of the kings.

Summer

SUMMER SOLSTICE (LITHIA)
June 20–22 (precise time varies every year)
Inspired by Brenda Hutchinson's continuing tenacity in her dailybell project

Background: Solstice means sun stopping. As the first day of summer, it is also the longest day of the year. It is when the North Pole tilts directly toward the sun, and when the sun's zenith is at its farthest point from the equator. Ceremonies are held throughout the world to acknowledge the phenomenon that the sun appears to rise and set, stop, and reverse direction on this day.

In the dailybell project, founder and New Music musician Brenda Hutchinson[7] rings bells every sunrise and sunset to make a daily observation of the sun every time it crosses the horizon.

To share that awareness with others, Brenda partakes in the summer solstice event at Chapel of the Chimes[8] in Oakland, California, in conjunction with New Music Bay Area.[9]

She works with a team on the open two levels of the mausoleum, greeting people from previous years who have brought their own bells, while distributing bells to newcomers. At the exact moment of the sunset, everyone is directed to rings the bells. Bell ringing goes on for twenty to thirty minutes. As a large participatory event, the solstice sunset bell ringing is now among the most exuberant and celebratory moments of the entire event.

Intention: Welcome in the summer. Find your tenacity and passion.

Question(s) to ask: How do I find the tenacity to do_____?

Special materials to bring: Bells, drums of all sizes, and other musical instruments

Other possibilities: Include an altar decorated with flowers, shells, and the bells; we are going to ring bells at the metaphorical or actual sunset. Hold the session someplace where you can face west and see the sun set. Bow or blow kisses to the sun. Offer the altar bells as gifts.

LAMMAS
August 1

Background: Lammas is the first of the harvest festivals. Grain has always been very important to mankind. Lammas translates to loaf mass, when the harvest flourishes. Lammas is the least celebrated of all the eight seasonal rituals. Since dancing has been a part of traditional Lammas festivals, I suggest to dance consciously in gratitude for everything we have.

Intention: To find community and personal strength

Question(s) to ask: What is illuminating me and how can I incorporate that into my life? What are my lessons for this summer?

Special materials to bring: Water bottles and fans. Pass around a bowl of fresh summer fruits such as berries. Bring potluck items for a barbecue following the class. Wear summer attire. Dance until you are out of breath and sweating.

Other possibilities: Include an altar decorated with strands of dried grasses, fresh fruits, and vegetables of all kinds. While eating the berries, imagine their nutrition filling your body. Invite participants to attend a communal barbecue with the intention of honoring summer. Continue with dancing into the night. Offer premade corn husk dolls.

Autumn

AUTUMN EQUINOX (MADON)
September 20–22 (precise time varies every year)

Background: Autumn equinox is the last celebration of the Celtic year. Like the spring equinox, the autumn equinox is the day when there is equal day and night, but instead of gaining more sunlight, we lose it. This is a time to honor the harvest and to find balance. Equinox is from the Latin words *aequus* (equal) and *nox* (night).

Intention: To find balance within. Turn over a new leaf.

Question(s) to ask: How can I weigh out these two things? Pull two cards, one for each object.

Special materials to bring: Two symbolic objects of what you would like to balance in your life. Or write them down on separate sheets of paper.

Examples: Snacks versus healthy food; bring a candy bar and a carrot.

A writing blockage versus agile writing; bring a dull pencil and a feather or fountain pen.

Other possibilities: Before asking the questions, hold symbolic objects, one in each hand, and have a guided or silent meditation, focusing on feeling the two in balance.
Use an old-fashioned weighing scale to weigh the two symbolic objects while speaking about what you'd like to balance, and why.
Include an altar with a cornucopia filled with dried herbs, acorns, and gourds for an altar. Offer colorful autumn leaves and acorns.

Trees respond by dropping leaves, the last harvest begins—grapes and fruits ripen to be made into spirits for winter storage of their energy and carbohydrates. The fresh love and hope of spring is completed—harvested and held in comfort through the winter.

—Ann Bridget Waters

ROSH HASHANAH AND YOM KIPPUR
September or October (both begin at sunset and are determined by the Jewish calendar)

Background: The high holidays, the Jewish New Year, Rosh Hashanah, and Yom Kippur, ten days later, are the holiest in the Jewish calendar. This is a time to ask forgiveness from God for all the mistakes and wrongdoing we have committed in the past year, so we will be written in the book of life for another year. It is also a time to remember our loved ones who have passed.

Intention: To understand the spiritual aspects of the Jewish New Year

General question to ask: How can I forgive_____? How can fix my wrongdoings?

Special materials to bring: On Rosh Hashanah, bring apples and honey to signify the imminent arrival of a sweet coming year. On Yom Kippur, bring small stones to throw in a nearby stream to represent ridding yourself of your sins.

Other possibilities: On Yom Kippur, fast from sunset to sunset the next day. Offer apples.

INDIGENOUS PEOPLES' DAY
Second Monday in October

Background: Indigenous Peoples' Day began in 1989 as a way of rethinking Columbus Day due to Christopher Columbus's history of colonizing America and his ill treatment of the Native American people.

Intention: To reclaim Columbus Day for indigenous people

General question to ask: How can I honor the indigenous people of my area?

Special materials to bring: Ritual objects representing indigenous cultures and the earth

Other possibilities: Include an altar decorated with objects found in nature. Research and discuss your local Native Americans.

SAMHAIN
October 31–November 1

Background: Taken from the Celts, Samhain marks the end of the current year and the beginning of the new one. It is a time to honor the dead, whose spirits were believed to roam the streets during this time. Costumes were worn to ward off evil spirits, and treats were left out to sweeten those spirits who might not ensure a good crop in the following year.

In Mexico, Samhain is also known as the Day of the Dead, when people create altars and visit the spirits of their ancestors who are dead. The celebrations have grown in popularity and become quite festive. Many of these altars and costumes are now recognized as fine works of art.

Intention: To make peace with our ancestors. To gain a more spiritual understanding of Halloween.

Special materials to bring: Photos of a deceased loved one, and memorial objects and thoughts of your ancestry in general

General question to ask: Direct your question to your deceased loved one or to your ancestry in general. What lesson can you teach me?

Other possibilities: Include an altar for photos and memorial objects. Discuss various viewpoints of death.

HALLOWEEN
October 31

Background: Halloween is the present-day holiday closely related to a seasonal celebration, Samhain. Halloween has evolved into dressing up in costumes and collecting sweets by going trick or treating.

Intention: To discover how the use of costumes affects our performances

General question to ask: What do I need to uncover?
Other possibilities: Include an altar decorated with pumpkins and Halloween images such as skeletons, goblins, and bats. Come dressed up as a chosen Tarot card. Have a Halloween party! Bring Halloween treats to share.

THANKSGIVING
Fourth Thursday in November

Background: Thanksgiving is purely a North American holiday that has no religious affiliations. First celebrated in 1621, Thanksgiving dates back to when the Pilgrims shared a feast with the native Indians to give thanks for their first bountiful harvest. Eventually Thanksgiving became a yearly celebration, and the Pilgrims also gave "thanks" for the foundation of the nation. The indigenous people saw Thanksgiving quite differently.

Intention: To expand personal gratitude to wishes for the world

General question to ask: What paradigm shift can I help create for my community or the world? How can I give back?

Special materials to bring: Thoughts on what you can do for the world

Other possibilities: Include an altar decorated with acorns, gourds, pumpkins, dried corncobs, and turkey feathers. For a "gratitude ritual," have everyone write, on three different pieces of paper, what they are grateful for spiritually, emotionally, and physically. Discuss and place in a hat, in a bowl, or on an altar. Collect food for the homeless. Offer acorns and cornbread.

I have laughed, cried and gained new insights about my life. The benefits have been physical and emotional. I felt more body integration of the new understandings. The classes are intimate yet sacred, personal yet shared in a safe space and with a private community, fun, serious, powerful and imaginative.

—Louise

CHAPTER VI

INTRODUCTION TO THE CARDS

Once I understood Tarot in my body,

then my mind could take it in.

—Valerie

Related symbols on the cards
serve as a structure
for movement pieces that encourage
you to come into your body,
change patterns, and deepen
realizations while having fun.

Historically, Tarot is known as a system of divination using a deck of seventy-eight cards. Opinions on their origins are diverse. Some speculate the Tarot may date back to ancient Egyptian culture and relates to the Tree of Life (Kabbalah). Tarot might have originally been a "Book of Wisdom" or a pictorial way for gypsies, who spoke different languages, to communicate. Others say the first deck may have been a wedding gift for the marriage of the Visconti and Sforza families in Italy during the Renaissance.

Tarot is unquestionably a pictorial version of the journey of life. Wherever Tarot originated, it has held the test of time because of its rich content.

After the Renaissance, as the Inquisition spread in Europe, the Tarot was considered a form of divination and was therefore outlawed, along with astrology, palm reading, and other oracular practices. In the early twentieth century, occult groups began to form, and new interpretations of Tarot decks appeared. Two different decks are now the basis for most modern Tarot decks: The Rider-Waite deck, (Rider being the publisher) was designed in 1910 by Arthur Edward Waite and illustrated by Pamela Coleman Smith. This Tarot deck gave pictorial images for every card. With artist Lady Frieda Harris, Aleister Crowley developed the Thoth deck in the 1940s. Crowley added astrological references for every card. Both decks came out of the Secret Society of the Golden Dawn in Britain.[1]

Tarot continues to evolve and take on new meaning. It has become a tool to help us gain clarity, make choices, and support our spiritual growth. There are countless versions of Tarot decks and books available today. As the desire for "knowing" grows, Tarot continues to become more and more mainstream.

Polarity Wellness Tarot (*PWT*) is the preferred deck to use to set up your Tarot in Motion dances because each card contains symbols that correlate to the guidelines included in this book.

The Tarot descriptions here may be used for individual Tarot card readings as well as for Tarot in Motion dances.

Each description includes the following information:

Meaning: A concise Tarot card interpretation to help guide you through your query

Elemental-movement qualities: Suits are correlated with elements that prompt you to understand their essential properties. A secondary element or subelement is provided to give you more options. Secondary elements are derived from the astrological aspects that relate to the card.

Dance pace: Quick, slow/ still, or moderate are suggested paces that might help you (at least) begin your dance. Paces are methodically derived from relating the card's given astrological signs to their seasonal placement.

Please note: Many of the pace suggestions are contradictory to the card meaning. Go with what feels best for you.
See the guidelines for more information.

Chakra: Using the original Vedic elemental names that relate to the Tarot suits. Chakra suggestions provide another dimension for understanding the cards.

Physical focus: Each *PWT* card includes an illustration of the physical body that highlights what part of the body is associated with this card. These associations are borrowed from Polarity Therapy.

Astrological influence: A brief description of the astrological and planetary signs that correspond to each card

Intention: An inspired intention to help give your dance a general purpose

Suggested moves and props: This section is meant to encourage your imagination. The information may assist you in picking up energy from each card to inspire your dance creation. You do not have to follow the suggested moves precisely.

Tarot alone can do the following:
Affirm your intuition
Point out possible choices along with their ramifications
Give clarification about what is going on
Reframe events you may feel you have no control over

The organization of the cards presented in *Tarot in Motion* are based on classic Tarot. By this I am referring to the popular Rider-Waite deck, illustrated by Pamela Colman Smith, which is the basis of many of the decks being made available. Astrological attributes are taken from the Thoth deck by Aleister Crowley and illustrated by Lady Frieda Harris. Although Crowley renames some of the cards and makes a few other changes, it is basically a classic deck. Physical focus and chakra references are taken from *PWT*.

From the seventy-eight-card Tarot deck, the typical deck of fifty-two playing cards is derived. Both decks have four suits. The playing deck has three court cards in each of the suits instead of the four court cards as in the Tarot. There is also a complete omission of the twenty-two cards known as the Major Arcana. Sometimes, although not often, the playing cards can be read.

Swords, representing your thoughts, are renamed spades. Wands, representing your insights, are renamed clubs. Cups, representing your emotions, are renamed hearts. Pentacles, representing the physical or material plane, are renamed diamonds.

Divisions of the Tarot

MAJOR ARCANA CARDS

Major Arcana cards are the twenty-two archetypical experiences in pictorial form. They usually show us the most important aspect of a reading. Major Arcana cards tend to point out the bigger picture.

The Major Arcana provide a more expansive view of the issue at hand. In a Tarot reading, the Majors point out our karmic lessons. These are influences you cannot change, although being made aware of them leads to tremendous insight. The Major Arcana are internal and spiritual matters.[2]

Each of the twenty-two Major Arcana cards have either an associated astrological sign or an associated planet. In the *PWT* deck, all Major Arcana cards relate to the ether element and ether/throat chakra. Here, I've organized the Major Arcana to include the third-eye and crown chakras.[2]

MINOR ARCANA CARDS

The forty Minor Arcana cards signify more of the details and the day-to-day issues. The Minors describe the possibilities of how things are or may play out in the real world. The Minor Arcana card suits are associated with the elements, and the chakras with their Vedic names. Each ace represents the pure essence of that suit/element/chakra. The cards numbered 2 through 10 have astrological references from Crowley or before that I've correlated with the esoteric anatomy of Polarity Therapy.

In this correlation, the astrology associations start with Aries at the forehead and end with Pisces at the feet.[3] See the chart in chapter III

COURT CARDS

There are sixteen court cards (pages, knights, queens, kings). The four court cards refer to specific people or to aspects of you that influence the issue at hand.

THE MEANING OF THE SUITS

The Minor Arcana, the number cards, and the court cards are broken up into the following suits.

 Swords/Air suit signifies a mental level of consciousness. These are our thoughts, ideas, trust, contemplations, and communication skills. Swords/Air cards are sometimes referred to as birds, or clouds. Movement, speed, and lightness are their characteristics. In modern times, the Swords/Air cards have become related to computers and correspondences. Swords/Air influence justice, harmony, and diplomacy.

 Wands/Fire suit signifies spirituality and creativity. These represent life force and intuition. They are also about spontaneity, strength, and power. Wands/Fire cards are sometimes referred to as rods, staffs, or batons. They are associated with focusing energy and the active, driving force behind anything we do.

 Cups/Water suit addresses our emotions, relationships, and human feelings. Cups/Water are mainly about love relationships. They signify connecting, flowing, and nurturing. Cups/Water cards are sometimes referred to as chalices or hearts. Cups/Water cards are often about the relationships of mother to child, between lovers, or, individually, about connecting our feet to the ground. They mirror our emotions. Cups/Water cards may also indicate the occult or addictions.

 Pentacle/Earth suit refers to everything physical, literal or material. They are about work, money issues, and structure. They put everything into practical perspective. Pentacle/Earth cards point out our physical needs and what is happening in our external world. Pentacle/Earth cards are sometimes referred to as disks or coins. A five-pointed star pattern often appears on these cards, symbolizing the human body. They signify stability and wealth.

In the healing process,
it is important to be seen.
It is often said that you need only
one witness in order to heal.

There is something in picking a Tarot card and focusing on it and then putting it to movement that is freeing. For several sessions I kept picking Sword cards; at this time, I was taking care of my mother, I keep trying to mentally figure out the best ways to take care of her. After her death, two times in a row I pulled the Chariot card! When I danced out the card, it felt wild and out of control. I could barely hold the reins. The second time I already felt much freer, and I was surprised at the transformation in my outlook toward her death. Both times I felt a growing feeling that I was charting a new direction with the Chariot card, and I was standing on my own.

—Carolyn

CHAPTER VII

THE MAJOR ARCANA CARDS

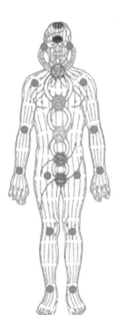

The Major Arcana cards narrate the entire range of archetypical experiences. The twenty-two cards also correspond to the twenty-two Hebrew letters and pathways of the Kabbalah (Tree of Life). They bring to our awareness archetypal or universal influences that we are currently experiencing, or soon will.

Expressive-movement qualities to use for the Major Arcana cards: Accepting, acknowledging, centered, elongated, expansive, grief, jealousy, listening, open, proud, silent, spiritual, sound, or spacey

The Major Arcana represent the joints in our body and the entire Astrological Wheel.

Card Meanings: The Fool through the World

0. Fool

Meaning: The Fool is spontaneous and seeks adventure. He is the archetypal wanderer. He tends to take risks. The Fool is fearless and willing to let everything go.

Expressive-movement qualities: Ether with air

Dance pace: Slow/still

Chakra: Ether/throat–space

Physical focus: Ankles

Astrologic influence: Uranus energy frees us from standard limitations and gives us new ideas.

Intention: Let go and take a leap of faith. Move without fear. Trust in the unknown wisdom.

Suggested moves and props: Be goofy. Jump and skip as if you were a child, or twirl in a circle. Dress in a crazy multicolored costume. Move out of the ordinary.

I. Magician

Meaning: The Magician has the ability to make something happen and has the correct tools for implementation. The Magician also indicates the ability to communicate.
Expressive-movement qualities: Ether with air
Dance pace: Moderate
Chakra: Ether/throat–space
Physical focus: Shoulders
Astrologic influence: Mercury rules expression and our ability to connect with others.
Intention: Use your imagination to manifest outcomes.
Suggested moves and props: Inhale through your nose to manifest what you want, and exhale out of your mouth all that you don't need. Include speaking. Use sacred objects representing a sword, a wand, a cup, and a pentacle.

II. High Priestess

Meaning: The High Priestess is the spiritual mother with psychic abilities. She indicates trusting and following your dreams. Although seemingly detached, she is aware of cycles and rhythms.
Expressive-movement qualities: Ether with water
Dance pace: Quick
Chakra: Ether/throat–space
Physical focus: Chest and heart
Astrologic influence: The moon energy is emotional, adaptable, and reflective.
Intention: Act on a hunch.
Suggested moves and props: Wear a robe or shawl. Follow your intuition. Go inward. Move like a comet and twirl around.

III. The Empress

Meaning: The Empress is Mother Earth and represents solid, abundant energy. The Empress is loving, caring, and secure. She is feminine power at its best.
Expressive-movement qualities: Ether with earth
Dance pace: Slow/still
Chakra: Ether/throat–space
Physical focus: Neck
Astrologic influence: Venus energy is about love, compassion, and connection. It is also about art and nature.
Intention: Take care of yourself as much as you take care of others.
Suggested moves and props: Wear a shawl and crown. Walk solidly, or stand still, with your hands open outward, adoring the Earth.

IV. The Emperor

Meaning: The Emperor is the quintessential father figure. He is assertive, extroverted, and established in a kind and fair way. The Emperor is a provider and has integrity.
Expressive-movement qualities: Ether with fire
Dance pace: Quick
Chakra: Ether/throat
Physical Focus: Forehead
Astrologic influence: Aries energy is active and assertive and enjoys starting things.
Intention: Take action into the world.
Suggested moves and props: Carry around a ruling stick. Wear a crown. Cross your arms. Move with solid footing. Do the yoga mountain pose.

V. The Hierophant

Meaning: The Hierophant exemplifies the traditional act of how we teach and learn. He likes to share knowledge. The Hierophant is a fundamentalist, who encompasses both tradition and law.
Expressive-movement qualities: Ether with earth
Dance pace: Slow/still
Chakra: Ether/throat
Physical focus: Throat
Astrologic influence: Taurus energy is secure, stubborn, and practical. It takes a long time to learn and then sticks with it.
Intention: Exchange knowledge. Become aware that everything is a lesson.
Suggested moves and props: Use a book as a prop. Stroke an imaginary beard. Explore every direction, connecting with others. Nod in understanding.

VI. The Lovers

Meaning: The Lovers point to a partnership with a lover, a business partner, or a project. Often the Lovers are a union of opposites who have a full understanding of each other.
Expressive-movement qualities: Ether with air
Dance pace: Moderate
Chakra: Ether/throat
Physical focus: Shoulders
Astrologic influence: Gemini energy is quick, light, and adaptable. It supports us to connect with others.
Intention: Open your heart in gratitude and love.
Suggested moves and props: Listen to your heartbeat while dancing with a partner, mimicking each other's moves. Hold and look at a stuffed animal amorously. Sing a love song.

VII. The Chariot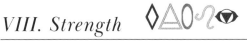

Meaning: The Chariot literally and metaphorically means taking the reins in your own hands and exercising your power. It is a calm and confident way of gaining control.
Expressive-movement qualities: Ether with water
Dance pace: Quick
Chakra: Ether/throat
Physical focus: Pelvis
Astrologic influence: Cancer energy is compassionate, sensitive, and nurturing. It is about love.
Intention: Acknowledge that you are on a ride and in control.
Suggested moves and props: Use a prop symbolic of a horse. Grab its pretend reins. Belly dance by showing flexibility, yet sturdiness from your core.

VIII. Strength

Meaning: Strength is another version of you "getting your act together," but with more outward force and intense focus than the Chariot. Strength is about taking control. It shows courage and dominance.
Expressive-movement qualities: Ether with fire
Dance pace: Slow/still
Chakra: Third eye
Physical focus: Belly
Astrologic influence: Leo energy is proud, dramatic, and adventurous. Leo insists on respect and appreciation.
Intention: Overcome all obstacles.
Suggested moves and props: On your hands and knees, mimic a lion or its tamer. Make roaring sounds.

IX. The Hermit

Meaning: The Hermit requires you to go within to gain spiritual awareness. He shows you coming to a spiritual understand by being in solitude. The Hermit is a sign that it is a good idea to meditate to find personal inner wisdom.
Expressive-movement qualities: Ether with earth
Dance pace: Quick
Chakra: Third eye
Physical focus: Lower abdomen
Astrologic influence: Virgo energy is meticulous, orderly, and detail oriented. It understands what's wrong and how to fix it. Virgo energy also has great connection to the out-of-doors.
Intention: Spend time alone in nature in order to find answers. Find your path on your own.
Suggested moves and props: Wear a blanket or scarf over your head. Carry a lantern, flashlight, or candle.

X. The Wheel of Fortune

Meaning: The Wheel indicates a turning of events. A change has come or will be coming for the better. It is jubilant time. The Wheel is lighthearted and sometimes unpredictable.
Expressive-movement qualities: Ether with fire
Dance pace: Slow/still
Chakra: Third eye
Physical focus: Thighs
Astrologic influence: Jupiter energy is truthful, optimistic, and expansive. You can be extremely powerful.
Intention: Acknowledge the changes in your life. Stay optimistic. Trust that everything always changes.
Suggested moves and props: Open your arms wide and move in all directions, creating a flow. Roll around a wheel or giant exercise ball.

XI. Justice

Meaning: Justice is reasonable, deliberate, and precise. Justice is neither kind nor cruel, whether it appears fair or not. It gives you the ability to weigh things out. This is the law of cause and effect. Justice encourages using diplomacy.
Expressive-movement qualities: Ether with air
Dance pace: Quick
Chakra: Third eye
Physical focus: Sides of the torso
Astrologic influence: Libra energy is balanced, truthful, and harmonious. It works well for fairness.
Intention: Contemplate every aspect of a pressing event or situation.
Suggested moves and props: Juggle two or three balls. Incorporate balancing various objects. Place each foot on two different surfaces.

XII. The Hanged Man

Meaning: The Hanged Man signifies a radical shift in perception. It shows the ability to look at the given situation in a new way, like viewing something from upside down. This card indicates a pattern disruption, possibly a radical change.
Expressive-movement qualities: Ether with water
Dance pace: Moderate
Chakra: Third eye
Physical focus: Feet
Astrologic influence: Neptune energy is spiritual and formless. It can be confusing or very useful if understood.
Intention: Look at things from a new perspective.
Suggested moves and props: Perform inversion yoga poses. Look at things from upside down. Throw objects (confetti?) up in the air and make a new pattern out of them.

XIII. Death

Meaning: The Death card indicates a loss or change of some kind. It rarely is an actual death. It is a shedding of an old way of being in order to prepare for something new to come in. The Death card is frightening only when it is resisted.

Expressive-movement qualities: Ether with water
Dance pace: Slow/still
Chakra: Third eye
Physical focus: Pelvis
Astrologic influence: Scorpio energy is passionate, deep, and intense. This energy can be negative, but if used correctly, it can give great power.
Intention: Embrace your transformation.
Suggested moves and props: Wear costumes of skeletons. Use snakelike props. Move in a way that you ordinarily would not move, and play with the pace.

XIV. Temperance

Meaning: Temperance is calm, contained, and balanced. Temperance indicates the presence of a healing angel. It exemplifies moderation and patience.

Expressive-movement qualities: Ether with fire
Dance pace: Moderate
Chakra: Third eye
Physical focus: Thighs
Astrologic influence: Sagittarius energy is idealistic, restless, and big-hearted. This helps us move to the future, and teaches us how to be balanced.
Intention: Act in moderation.
Suggested moves and props: Place each foot on two different surfaces. Wear angel wings and androgynous clothing.

XV. The Devil

Meaning: The Devil can be either superficial or self-indulgent. He has a tendency toward addictions. He asks to look beyond surface appearances. On the other hand, the Devil is a rascal, which can be charming.

Expressive-movement qualities: Ether with earth
Dance pace: Quick
Chakra: Crown
Physical focus: Knees
Astrologic influence: Capricorn energy is cautious, structured, and self-controlled. Capricorn energy helps manage work that needs to be done.
Intention: Look past the surface for deeper meaning. Let go of your obsessions.
Suggested moves and props: Become a trickster. Act alternatingly like you've overindulged and then come to your senses. Wear pretend devil ears. While dancing, announce each step.

XVI. The Tower

Meaning: The Tower shows a breaking down of all defenses and boundaries. It is an upheaval and gives everyone a bolt of insight to establish a new pattern. The Tower is destructive only if we allow it to be.
Expressive-movement qualities: Ether with fire
Dance pace: Quick
Chakra: Crown
Physical focus: Forehead
Astrologic influence: Mars energy can be upsetting because it is so powerful, but with awareness may encourage drive and courage.
Intention: Be present when things fall apart. Set a new intention with deep feeling.
Suggested moves and props: Build a structure out of available materials and then push it over. Throw blocks or bunched-up paper. Intermittently, gently fall to the ground and get up.

XVII. The Star

Meaning: The Star is where dreams come into fruition. It is an acknowledgment of optimism and spiritual regeneration. The Star is shining in glory. She is at peace and inspired.
Expressive-movement qualities: Ether with air
Dance pace: Moderate
Chakra: Crown
Physical focus: Ankles
Astrologic influence: Aquarius energy is individualistic, trendsetting, and extreme. New ideas and plans can go very well.
Intention: Expand your charismatic field. Feel the radiance flowing through your body.
Suggested moves and props: Lift your head up high. Allow the glow of yourself to flow through you. Stretch out your arms in a star pose.

XVIII. The Moon

Meaning: The Moon indicates a trust in intuition and reflects on our dreams. It illuminates the darkness, accessing deep, subconscious levels of intuition and psychic knowing.
Expressive-movement qualities: Ether with water
Dance pace: Slow/still
Chakra: Crown
Physical focus: Feet
Astrologic influence: Pisces energy is idealistic and compassionate. At times, Pisces energy is psychic and spiritual.
Intention: Listen to your dreams. Get in touch with the unknown.
Suggested moves and props: Light one candle with care and meditate in the dark.

XVIX. The Sun

Meaning: The Sun tells of pure happiness and being in a truly wonderful place. It exemplifies confidence, health, and vitality.
Expressive-movement qualities: Ether with fire
Dance pace: Slow/still
Chakra: Crown
Physical focus: Belly
Astrologic influence: Sun energy is ego-identified, radiant, and outgoing. It is about your personal nature.
Intention: Feel the power of being in a fantastic place.
Suggested moves and props: Use the entire space. Look upward. Throw metaphoric kisses up toward the sun. Do a yoga sun salutation, if you know how. Show your gratitude with a large, ecstatic grin.

XX. Judgment

Meaning: Judgment is an awakening to something we have not seen before, which may be exciting or shocking. Judgment is a paradigm shift with the essence of a revelation. Judgment is an angel of resurrection.
Expressive-movement qualities: Ether with water
Dance pace: Slow/still
Chakra: Crown
Physical focus: Pelvis
Astrologic influence: Pluto is transformative, regenerative, and subversive. Pluto is the energy of letting go of what doesn't work.
Intention: Become aware of the cosmic forces at hand.
Suggested moves and props: Use a shiny light and beat a drum. Act surprised.

XXI. The World

Meaning: The World card represents the ultimate experience. It indicates the place where you most are aligned with Spirit. It is where all our dreams are fulfilled.
Expressive-movement qualities: Ether with earth
Dance pace: Moderate
Chakra: Crown
Physical focus: Knees
Astrologic influence: Saturn energy is orderly, disciplined, and transcending. It helps us work hard and manage others.
Intention: Dance on your limitations.
Suggested moves and props: Dance as if you've never danced before. Shake rattles. Rotate an open umbrella. Verbally express your joy.

Patricia danced for a ballet company during the early '60s. She admits at first she had resistance to creating dance from a Tarot card and in front of the other participants. It took her time to get use to creating a free-form dance. She now pulls a card and dances it for herself every day. Patricia says, "I'm learning Tarot in an entirely new way."

CHAPTER VIII

THE AIR/SWORD CARDS

Tarot in Motion builds a beautiful and reassuring case for us to communicate through dance.

—Holly

Air/Sword cards signify everything mental. They are our thoughts, ideas, contemplations, and communication skills.

Air/Sword cards are about logic and the way we internalize negative and positive thinking. Since Air is the lightest of all the elements, Air/Swords are the easiest to change. The Air/Sword suite is about the way we make decisions and the ways in which we think. In modern times, Air relates to computers and technology.

Expressive-movement qualities to use for Air/Sword cards:
Bargaining, brilliant, caring, charitable, compassionate, considering, desirous, empathetic, envious, examining, fast, giddy, high-strung, jittery, joyful, jumpy, talkative, laughing, judging, or quick witted.

Astrological Air Signs and the Body

Gemini	shoulders
Libra	kidneys
Aquarius	ankles

Ace of Air/Swords

Meaning: All aces signify a new beginning. The Ace of Air indicates a new, clear thought or perspective. It signifies inspired ideas with easily reached solutions. The Ace of Air is very focused. It indicates the moment when the figurative lightbulb goes off and illuminates your thoughts.
Expressive-movement qualities: Pure air
Dance pace: Slow/still
Chakra: Air/heart—compassion
Physical focus: Shoulders, kidneys, and ankles
Astrologic influence: All air signs: Gemini, Libra, and Aquarius
Intention: Find a swift, determined breakthrough.
Suggested moves and props: Have a fan blowing toward you. Stand still, with one hand shading your eyes. With the other hand, hold a sword away from the body, looking at it in awe.

Two of Air/Swords

Meaning: Two of Air is balanced, clear, and still. There is harmony in the presence of the Two of Swords. It indicates a calm, accepting peace of mind. It also may indicate holding two disparate or contradictory ideas as true and valid at the same time.
Expressive-movement qualities: Air with water
Dance pace: Rapid
Chakra: Air/heart—compassion
Physical focus: Sides of the torso
Astrologic influence: Moon in Libra signifies the justice and equality that is best for all.
Intention: Be willing to wait for more information to arrive before acting.
Suggested moves and props: Do spinal twists. Close your eyes while moving in harmony. Make a Sufi-like dance.

Three of Air/Swords

Meaning: The Three of Air suggests a feeling of loss, disappointment, or confusion. It signifies depressive thoughts that fuel anguish. Three of Air shows being in a state of failing confidence or being in a state of despair.
Expressive-movement qualities: Air with fire
Dance pace: Quick
Chakra: Air/heart—compassion
Physical focus: Sides of the torso
Astrologic influence: Saturn in Libra can cause frustration and a desire to find a middle ground and compromise. It invites us to be objective.
Intention: Be open to loving help.
Suggested moves and props: Breathe into your lungs and chest. Take a stance that opens your heart. Place your hands on hips and move from left to right.

Four of Air/Swords

Meaning: The Four of Air shows that you are in a period of retreating and waiting. It requires you to slow down, and even to hide out in order to regenerate and organize. The Four of Air indicates being patient and well rested.
Expressive-movement qualities: Air with earth
Dance pace: Quick
Chakra: Air/heart–compassion
Physical focus: Sides of the torso
Astrologic influence: Jupiter in Libra is magnificent benevolence, loving nobility. It leans toward balance and equality.
Intention: Withdraw in order to recover. Be accepting of resting.
Suggested moves and props: Breathe mindfully. Recline on cushions. Set up a sanctuary.

Five of Air/Swords

Meaning: All Fives–regardless of suit–are turning points. The Five of Air is thinking you've failed when you are really at a point of transition. It shows a battle not worth fighting. The Five of Air tells you that giving up is not a failure.
Expressive-movement qualities: Air with earth
Dance pace: Slow/still
Chakra: Air/heart–compassion
Physical focus: Ankles and calves
Astrologic influence: Venus in Aquarius values all people. It is about knowing when to give up, and that we learn from our failures.
Intention: Drop the situation at hand. Move on and trust.
Suggested moves and props: Walk back and forth or in circles, flinging arms about in frustration. Stop suddenly and take in the wondering, "What if I quit?"

Six of Air/Swords

Meaning: The Six of Air is safe, serene, and focused. It is moving away from danger to calmer understandings. The Six of Air influence accepts help from others. It looks forward and is optimistic about the future. New opportunities are ahead.
Expressive-movement qualities: Air with air
Dance pace: Slow/still
Chakra: Air/heart–compassion
Physical focus: Ankles and calves
Astrologic influence: Mercury in Aquarius communicates higher information, often in the form of reality versus illusion. This may indicate being out of touch with your emotions.
Intention: Fully accept help and guidance.
Suggested moves and props: Pretend to be rowing a boat, moving away from danger. One person guides another gently. Use scarves swaying close to the ground.

Seven of Air/Swords

Meaning: The Seven of Air is either self-protective or sneaky. At times it may even appear selfish due to taking on too many responsibilities. The Seven of Air shows an aspect of self-sufficiency. It brings up issues of trust and worthiness that take courage.
Expressive-movement qualities: Air with water
Dance pace: Slow/still
Chakra: Air/heart—compassion
Physical focus: Ankles and calves
Astrologic influence: Moon in Aquarius is comfortable with innovation and new ideas. It shows that you are your own person.
Intention: Too much self-sufficiency leads to lack of trust.
Suggested moves and props: Begin with coming out from hiding in a corner. Crawl around carefully, not allowing others get in the way.

Eight of Air/Swords

Meaning: The Eight of Air shows being trapped in thoughts to the point of being blinded by them. The Eight of Air encourages being open to other points of view.
Expressive-movement qualities: Air with earth
Dance pace: Moderate
Chakra: Air/heart—compassion
Physical focus: Shoulders
Astrologic influence: Jupiter in Gemini pushes us to think out of the box. It encourages us to grow and expand mentally.
Intention: Surrender your mental process in order to grow spiritually.
Suggested moves and props: Begin by being tied up and blindfolded, then unwrap yourself. Have others surround you in a tight knit circle as you figure your way out.

Nine of Air/Swords

Meaning: The Nine of Air recognizes negative mind chatter, self-blame, or doubt, even to the point of suffering. It indicates the condition of overobsessing on fearful, negative, or anxious thoughts, to the point where those thoughts start to infiltrate your dreams.
Expressive-movement qualities: Air with fire
Dance pace: Moderate
Chakra: Air/heart—compassion
Physical focus: Shoulders
Astrologic influence: Mars in Gemini can give us vitality yet also may lack focus, sometimes leaving a project incomplete. It can cause a lack of stability.
Intention: Remember, worrying is like paying for something negative to happen.
Suggested moves and props: Lie on your back while flaying your arms and legs. Yell out self-criticism and what is bothering you until it sounds silly.

Ten of Air/Swords △⊖⊙⊙Ⅱ✹

Meaning: All Tens–whatever the suite–are an ending. The Ten of Air is overly dramatic and describes the perception of a completely devastating situation unfolding in your life. It signifies a sense of defeat and ruin. If these obsessive thoughts are released, something new can come in.
Expressive-movement qualities: Air with fire
Dance pace: Moderate
Chakra: Air/heart–compassion
Physical focus: Shoulders to open arms
Astrologic influence: Sun in Gemini inspires you to expand your understanding and detach from being overly emotional. It suggests that you be curious about everything around you.
Intention: Calm down so you know what to do next.
Suggested moves and props: Play out your overdramatized situation. Pretend to stab yourself. Shrug your shoulders as if you are rolling your troubles off your back.

Page of Air/Swords △0▽✹

Meaning: The Page of Air refers to another person or an aspect of yourself that is influencing the situation by having a new idea. The Page of Air communicates his/her idea in a clear, articulate fashion. He encourages you to speak your truth.
Expressive-movement qualities: Air with earth
Dance pace: Slow/still
Chakra: Air/heart–compassion
Physical focus: Shoulders, kidneys, and ankles
Astrologic influence: All air signs: Gemini, Libra, and Aquarius
Intention: Communicate your new idea.
Suggested moves and props: Pretend to text, while speaking out loud.

Knight of Air/Swords △⊕△✹

Meaning: The Knight of Air refers to another person or an aspect of yourself that is influencing the situation by taking action. The Knight of Air takes a logical stance with clear intent. He can support you by analyzing situations. At times he is not connected to his feelings and can even be hasty.
Expressive-movement qualities: Air with fire
Dance pace: Quick
Chakra: Air/heart–compassion
Physical focus: Shoulders, kidneys, and ankles
Astrologic influence: All air signs: Gemini, Libra, and Aquarius
Intention: Cut through all obstacles. Be objective.
Suggested moves and props: Practice a martial art. Charge ahead on a pretend horse.

Queen of Air/Swords

Meaning: The Queen of Air refers to another person or an aspect of yourself that is influencing the situation in an objective yet fair way. The Queen of Air puts her emotions aside and doesn't mince words. She can help you find clarity.
Expressive-movement qualities: Air with water
Dance pace: Moderate
Chakra: Air/heart–compassion
Physical focus: Shoulders, kidneys, and ankles
Astrologic influence: All air signs: Gemini, Libra, and Aquarius
Intention: Be objective and earnest.
Suggested moves and props: Wear a queen's crown and robe. Take a still stance while holding a sword. Find eye contact with others. Act with serious self-control.

King of Air/Swords

Meaning: The King of Air refers to another person or an aspect of yourself that is influencing the situation in a paternal or leadership way. The King of Air is cool headed and focused. He is an intellectual and communicates with confidence and integrity. He makes his decisions from an objective basis.
Expressive-movement qualities: Air with air
Dance pace: Quick
Chakra: Air/heart–compassion
Physical focus: Shoulders, kidneys, and ankles
Astrologic influence: All air signs: Gemini, Libra, and Aquarius
Intention: Think in an objective and intelligent manner.
Suggested moves and props: March to drum music, while focusing seriously on a target. Carry a sword. Speak as if you're teaching others, in an unemotional and informative voice.

CHAPTER IX

THE FIRE/WAND CARDS

I liked that the space didn't feel very intimidating. I felt I could speak openly and freely for the most part, and I really appreciated that. Being outside seemed to be a more effective way to connect, communicate, and create. I liked the warming-up part before getting involved with the Tarot readings. The usage of props was cool, and I found that to be very helpful to me.

—*Karen*

Fire/Wand cards are about everything spiritual and creative. These cards are associated with the passion behind our ability to take action.

Fire/Wand cards show us spontaneity, vision, and intuition. They also indicate being outgoing and charismatic. They focus our energy to burn, which at times needs to be tempered.

Expressive-movement qualities for Fire/Wand cards: Active, angry, bright, controlling, creative, charismatic, dominant, enthusiastic, forgiving, frustrating, persuasive, potent, powerful, resentful, shaking, thrilled, vital, or willful

Astrological Fire Signs and the Body

Aries	forehead
Leo	solar plexus
Sagittarius	thighs

Ace of Fire/Wands

Meaning: All aces represent a new beginning. The Ace of Fire is a powerful seed of creativity and spiritual well-being. This ace is forceful and passionate. It sets your spirit into motion and inspires new creative directions.
Expressive-movement qualities: Pure fire
Dance pace: Slow/still
Chakra: Fire/solar plexus—drive
Physical focus: Forehead, solar plexus, and thighs
Astrologic influence: All fire signs: Aries, Leo, and Sagittarius
Intention: Start a creative endeavor.
Suggested moves and props: Use a magic wand or a broomstick. Enthusiastically prance around. Light a candle.

Two of Fire/Wands

Meaning: The Two of Fire is a place of germination that keeps a project going. It is spiritually looking in the correct direction. The Two of Fire exemplifies beauty, kindness, and passion.
Expressive-movement qualities: Fire with fire
Dance pace: Quick
Chakra: Fire/solar plexus—drive
Physical focus: Forehead and eyes
Astrologic influence: Mars in Aries is about energy. Since Mars rules Aries, it heightens a force behind the concept of an idea. This influences you in what to do to get yourself going.
Intention: Make a bold choice.
Suggested moves and props: Beat a drum. Rapidly walk in an infinity sign. Move with your head held high.

Three of Fire/Wands

Meaning: The Three of Fire is a manifestation and assessment of what has already been implemented. It is the outcome of an action. The Three of Fire evaluates progress before moving forward. An important part of the creative process is being able to see past patterns, and also evaluating what has worked and what hasn't.
Expressive-movement qualities: Fire with fire
Dance pace: Quick
Chakra: Fire/solar plexus—drive
Physical focus: Forehead and eyes
Astrologic influence: The pure essence of sun in Aries is what we have achieved. It is a sparkle of vitality.
Intention: Stick with the repeated pattern that works.
Suggested moves and props: Use a handheld telescope. Look up and down, behind and ahead. Run in a spiral. Repeat any movement pattern.

Four of Fire/Wands

Meaning: The Four of Fire is celebratory and complete. It indicates the sharing of joy while relaxing. It is being at ease with how things are developing. Four of Fire is stable and confident, indicating the external expression of success.
Expressive-movement qualities: Fire with earth
Dance pace: Quick
Chakra: Fire/solar plexus–drive
Physical focus: Forehead and eyes
Astrologic influence: Venus in Aries shows a loving attraction, compassion, and connections. It signifies a joyous future.
Intention: Recognize your progress.
Suggested moves and props: Dance by moving in and out of a square formed by the placement of four staves or candles. Include yellow, orange, and red scarves.

Five of Fire/Wands

Meaning: All Fives are turning points. The Five of Fire is about mustering the courage to overcome obstacles. It is clever, forceful, and strategic and has an element of enjoying the challenge. The Five of Fire releases pent-up energy. It indicates the ability to strive and sustain a given situation.
Expressive-movement qualities: Fire with fire
Dance pace: Slow/still
Chakra: Fire/solar plexus–drive
Physical focus: Belly
Astrologic influence: Saturn in Leo is about doing your own thing creatively while still including others.
Intention: Have fun turning your challenges into opportunities.
Suggested moves and props: Pretend playful martial arts moves.

Six of Fire/Wands

Meaning: The Six of Fire denotes success after working extremely hard. This is initiating leadership and coming out ahead. You have won. Receiving this card acknowledges your accomplishments.
Expressive-movement qualities: Fire with earth
Dance pace: Slow/still
Chakra: Fire/solar plexus–drive
Physical focus: Belly
Astrologic influence: Jupiter in Leo gives you warmth in your soul. It indicates having faith with grace and optimism. Jupiter in Leo brings good fortune.
Intention: Embrace your success.
Suggested moves and props: Shimmy and undulate with arm up and legs wide apart. Jump for joy. As you move, smile from deep inside your body.

Seven of Fire/Wands

Meaning: Seven of Fire signifies maintaining and standing up for your beliefs. It tells of moving with courage and defiance. The Seven of Fire is also eccentric and very powerful. It shows standing up for what you believe in.
Expressive-movement qualities: Fire with fire
Dance pace: Slow/still
Chakra: Fire/solar plexus–drive
Physical focus: Belly
Astrologic influence: With Mars in Leo, Mars has drive, desire, and courage. Mars brings strong will and passion to Leo, which is already very powerful.
Intention: Stand in your truth with courage. Follow your gut feeling.
Suggested moves and props: Lower and rise from a squat position, stomp around, hold your head up high. Punch the air.

Eight of Fire/Wands

Meaning: The Eight of Fire indicates moving rapidly with unfocused passion. It is unconscious and fervent. It means releasing energy into action. The Eight of Fire is intuitive and free.
Expressive-movement qualities: Fire with air
Dance pace: Moderate
Chakra: Fire/solar plexus–drive
Physical focus: Thighs
Astrologic influence: Mercury in Sagittarius has the ability to communicate a vision of what is best for all concerned. It also shows a continual search for meaning.
Intention: Be inspired by random spurts of energy.
Suggested moves and props: Dance in zigzag directions, while shaking rattles.

Nine of Fire/Wands

Meaning: Nine of Fire is accomplished, successful, and often exhausting. It indicates endurance, resilience, and proven success. It is both internal and external accomplishments. The Nine of Fire indicates driven and dynamic energy.
Expressive-movement qualities: Fire with water
Dance pace: Moderate
Chakra: Fire/solar plexus–drive
Physical focus: Thighs
Astrologic influence: Sun and Moon in Sagittarius indicates being radiant and needing to be alone. At the same time, the Sun in Sagittarius is seeing a vision and manifesting it in life. The Moon in Sagittarius is about honesty and adventure.
Intention: Wind down your efforts.
Suggested moves and props: Burn a candle at both ends (or pretend to). Incorporate using a flashlight. From sitting on your heels, rise as if in a plié.

Ten of Fire/Wands

Meaning: All Tens are an ending. Ten of Fire brings satisfying success, often accompanied by exhaustion. It is both internal and external accomplishment. The Ten of Fire shows that you have emerged on the other side. You may even have a few scars or wounds to prove it. It shows passion behind an all-encompassing endeavor.
Expressive-movement qualities: Fire with fire
Dance pace: Moderate
Chakra: Fire/solar plexus–drive
Physical focus: Thighs
Astrologic influence: Saturn in Sagittarius is the ability to ground and manifest on earth. Sagittarius is the future.
Intention: Lift off the weight of your burdens.
Suggested moves and props: Hold many items such as batons or sticks and drop them. Stride off with your head held high.

Page of Fire/Wands

Meaning: The Page of Fire refers to another person or an aspect of yourself that is influencing the situation by being enthusiastic and young spirited. The Page of Fire is young and confident. She/he is filled with excitement about seeking a new creative idea or spiritual path.
Expressive-movement qualities: Fire with earth
Dance pace: Slow/still
Chakra: Fire/solar plexus–drive
Physical focus: Forehead, solar plexus, and thighs
Astrologic influence: All fire signs: Aries, Leo, and Sagittarius
Intention: Follow Spirit and see where it leads you.
Suggested moves and props: In a childlike way, explore looking around with wonder and eagerness. Do a breakdance.

Knight of Fire/Wands

Meaning: The Knight of Fire refers to another person or an aspect of yourself that is influencing the situation by charging ahead without warning in a gust of passion. The Knight is filled with confidence and loves adventure. She/he tends to be daring and fearless.
Expressive-movement qualities: Fire with fire
Dance pace: Quick
Chakra: Fire/solar plexus–drive
Physical focus: Solar plexus
Astrologic influence: All fire signs: Aries, Leo, and Sagittarius
Intention: Stay sharp, charismatic, and energetic.
Suggested moves and props: Disco dance or pretend to ride a horse while holding a rod.

Queen of Fire/Wands

Meaning: The Queen of Fire refers to another person or an aspect of yourself that is influencing the situation with passion for creativity and spirituality. The Queen of Fire knows what she wants and knows how to get it. You cannot deter her. She tends to be very creative and passionate about whatever it is she's doing. She is honest and blunt.
Expressive-movement qualities: Fire with water
Dance pace: Moderate
Chakra: Fire/solar plexus–drive
Physical focus: Forehead, solar plexus, and thighs
Astrologic influence: All fire signs: Aries, Leo, and Sagittarius
Intention: Be comfortable with your assertiveness.
Suggested moves and props: Wear a queen's crown and sexy clothing. Shake your hips and thighs. Dance with scarves.

King of Fire/Wands

Meaning: The King of Fire refers to another person or an aspect of yourself that is influencing the situation in a paternal or leadership way. He indicates having a passionate and courageous temperament. He is a real fighter and has a vision. The King of Fire is an inspirational, powerful leader. He is bold and confident.
Expressive-movement qualities: Fire with earth
Dance pace: Quick
Chakra: Fire/solar plexus–drive
Physical focus: Forehead, solar plexus, and thighs
Astrologic influence: All fire signs: Aries, Leo, and Sagittarius
Intention: Come into your own power.
Suggested moves and props: Wear a crown and robe. Hold a torch. Get others to follow you.

CHAPTER X

THE WATER/CUP CARDS

I found while dancing the card I pulled, the lesson of patience became more obtainable and I was able to look at the bigger picture of my present situation.

—Sandra

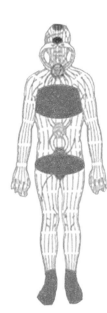

Water/Cup cards are about human emotions and relationships. They signify connecting, flowing, and being nurturing with loved ones and others, and even possibly with inanimate objects.

Water connects the mother to the child, adults to their sexuality, and our feet to the ground. Water/Cup cards indicate psychic abilities and addictions. They convey our ability to be receptive and be flexible. They also recognize a need for boundaries.

Expressive-movement qualities for Water/Cup cards: Accepting, addictive, belonging, bonding, boundaryless, compulsive, connecting, emotional, flowing, fluid, kind, loving, nurturing, overbearing, sensual, sensitive, sexy, or smooth

Astrological Water Signs and the Body

Cancer	chest
Scorpio	pelvis
Pisces	feet

Ace of Water/Cups

Meaning: All aces are a new beginning. The Ace of Water indicates a new love, any kind of love—friendly, parental, or romantic. It is a new way of feeling and is the source of anything psychic. This ace suggests flow.
Expressive-movement qualities: Pure water
Dance pace: Slow/still
Chakra: Water/sexual chakra—flowing
Physical focus: Chest, pelvis, and feet
Astrologic influence: All water signs: Cancer, Scorpio, and Pisces
Intention: Open your heart.
Suggested moves and props: Hold a cup, water bottle, or bowl in both hands up to your heart as an offering.

Two of Water/Cups

Meaning: The Two of Water shows an opening of the heart to another person or a thing. It is a merging of some kind with another. It could be a romantic adventure. Two of Water indicates a karmic relationship. This is the beginning of an intimate relationship, or a friendship, or a mother-to-child connection.
Expressive-movement qualities: Water with earth
Dance pace: Quick
Chakra: Water/sexual chakra—flowing
Physical focus: Chest
Astrologic influence: Venus in Cancer shows us the importance of home, beauty, and loving relationships. It calls for reciprocity.
Intention: Expand your love to others.
Suggested moves and props: With two people, take turns mirroring each other. Incorporate shimmying from your chests.

Three of Water/Cups ▽⊕☿♀♋◎

Meaning: The Three of Water communicates and celebrates with friends. It is playful. It points out a joyous connection with others.
Expressive-movement qualities: Water with air
Dance pace: Quick
Chakra: Water/sexual chakra—flowing
Physical focus: Chest
Astrologic influence: Mercury in Cancer provides us with great intuition for other people's feelings. It is the remembering of emotions.
Intention: Create a goddess party.
Suggested moves and props: Participate in a contact improv-type dance. Move facing a mirror. Dance closely in a group while passing scarves. Imagine or actually pour water from three different vessels, into each other.

Four of Water/Cups

Meaning: The Four of Water is still, stable, and safe. At times it is a bit detached in order to remain objective as a protective measure. The Four of Water ranges from feeling comfortable, even luxurious, to stagnant and apathetic.
Expressive-movement qualities: Water with water
Dance pace: Quick
Chakra: Water/sexual chakra–flowing
Physical focus: Chest
Astrologic influence: Moon in Cancer calms down our emotions. It either provides safety or can feel like a wall around our emotions. Moon in Cancer shows a need for cautiousness.
Intention: Become aware of your emotional safety. Make sure you are safe but not detached from your feelings.
Suggested moves and props: Put on gloves and shake them off. Sit or stand sideways to the audience, look at them, and then look away. Connecting, then detaching.

Five of Water/Cups

Meaning: All Fives are turning points. The Five of Water brings your disappointments to the surface. It brings an awareness of feeling lonely and futile so you can turn your thoughts beneficially.
Expressive-movement qualities: Water with fire
Dance pace: Slow/still
Chakra: Water/sexual chakra–flowing
Physical focus: Pelvis
Astrologic influence: Mars in Scorpio directs the action to go very deep, which may be the drive to change or turning a corner.
Intention: Place an emphasis on hope.
Suggested moves and props: Walk to a chosen location in the room; do a few hip circles. Then turn and go to another location. Repeat sequence five times.

Six of Water/Cups

Meaning: The Six of Water is all about imparting out of love and charity. It is trusting in a mutual exchange. Six of Water is filled with kindness and gratitude.
Expressive-movement qualities: Water with fire
Dance pace: Slow/still
Chakra: Water/sexual chakra–flowing
Physical focus: Pelvis
Astrologic influence: The Sun in Scorpio helps us find our hidden secrets and dig beneath the surface. It helps our mysteries come into focus. The sun in Scorpio gives us fierce loyalty to those we are committed to.
Intention: The love you take is equal to the love you make.
Suggested moves and props: Wrap scarves and Hawaiian leis around another participant. Continue to tenderly caress them. Sway from your hips. Give away roses.

Seven of Water/Cups

Meaning: The Seven of Water shows harmless fantasies, filled with hope, that help us dream big for the sake of obtaining higher dreams. On the other hand, the Seven of Water at times indicates self-indulgent emotional states to the point of debauchery.
Expressive-movement qualities: Water with earth
Dance pace: Slow/still
Chakra: Water/sexual chakra—flowing
Physical focus: Pelvis
Astrologic influence: Venus in Scorpio gets below the surface of your dreams and desires. Venus is the energy love. Scorpio brings on intensity, causing your love to have a fierce commitment.
Intention: Reach for something better than you ever imagined.
Suggested moves and props: From a resting pose, hold a vessel up to the sky and undulate like a snake upward. Reach toward it and jump at the same time.

Eight of Water/Cups

Meaning: The Eight of Water indicates the ability to walk away from an emotionally charged situation. It shows a process of overgiving to the point of exhaustion and becoming inert. The Eight of Water brings an awareness of the need to set boundaries for the sake of self-preservation.
Expressive-movement qualities: Water with earth
Dance pace: Moderate
Chakra: Water/sexual chakra—flowing
Physical focus: Feet
Astrologic influence: Saturn in Pisces gives us time to look inward. It allows us to dream and plan. It is about sacrificing anything and withstanding difficulties.
Intention: Know when to walk away.
Suggested moves and props: Gather up objects and place them neatly in a pile in one corner. Pretend to bid your objects farewell and walk away heel to toe.

Nine of Water/Cups

Meaning: The Nine of Water affirms satisfaction and fulfilled dreams. The Nine of Water is about being physically and emotionally healthy. It is tangible happiness.
Expressive-movement qualities: Water with fire
Dance pace: Moderate
Chakra: Water/sexual chakra—flowing
Physical focus: Feet
Astrologic influence: Jupiter in Pisces shows a deep compassion for spirituality. It expands your faith.
Intention: Acknowledge the joy in your life.
Suggested moves and props: Walk on tiptoes while performing a belly-like dance. Include rolling movements of the abdomen. Smile.

Ten of Water/Cups

Meaning: All Tens signal an ending. The Ten of Water is complete contentment and joy. It shows up in all aspects of our lives and can be shared with others. The Ten of Water radiates outward with bliss.
Expressive-movement qualities: Water with fire
Dance pace: Moderate
Chakra: Water/sexual chakra—flowing
Physical focus: Feet
Astrologic influence: Mars in Pisces creates the feeling of being content, although Mars and Pisces have conflicting energies.
Intention: Appreciate the overflow of abundance.
Suggested moves and props: Invite participants to follow you in walking in a circle, holding hands and pressing your feet into the floor.

Page of Water/Cups

Meaning: The Page of Water is another person or an aspect of you influencing the situation by having youthful energy filled with expectations of love and intimacy. She/he is flirtatious and affectionate.
Expressive-movement qualities: Water with earth
Dance pace: Slow/still
Chakra: Water/sexual chakra—flowing
Physical focus: Chest, pelvis, and feet
Astrologic influence: All water signs: Cancer, Scorpio, and Pisces
Intention: Remember your first romantic love.
Suggested moves and props: Act flirtatiously. Read a love poem out loud.

Knight of Water/Cups

Meaning: The Knight of Water is another person or an aspect of you that is influencing the situation by being a romantic visionary.
Expressive-movement qualities: Water with fire
Dance pace: Quick
Chakra: Water/sexual chakra—flowing
Physical focus: Chest, pelvis, and feet
Astrologic influence: All water signs: Cancer, Scorpio, and Pisces
Intention: Hold that romantic vision in your mind.
Suggested moves and props: Do a version of salsa dancing. Clack castanets.

Queen of Water/Cups

Meaning: The Queen of Water is another person or an aspect of you that is influencing the situation by being loving and understanding. She is very intuitive and self-aware.
Expressive-movement qualities: Water with water
Dance pace: Moderate
Chakra: Water/sexual chakra—flowing
Physical focus: Chest, pelvis, and feet
Astrologic influence: All water signs: Cancer, Scorpio, and Pisces
Intention: Be warm and kind.
Suggested moves and props: Wear a queen's crown and heavy cloche. Instigate a group hug.

King of Water/Cups

Meaning: The King of Water is another person or an aspect of yourself that is influencing the situation in a paternal or leadership way. He is aware of his own feelings and considers the feelings of others before making a decision. The King of Water accepts people for who they are.
Expressive-movement qualities: Water with fire
Dance pace: Quick
Chakra: Water/sexual chakra—flowing
Physical focus: Chest, pelvis, and feet
Astrologic influence: All water signs: Cancer, Scorpio, and Pisces
Intention: May love become our religion.
Suggested moves and props: Lead a line dance, winding back and forth, ending up in a circle.

CHAPTER XI

THE EARTH/PENTACLE CARDS

The cards help me get back into my physical body. I learn something new about myself every time.

—Jennifer

Earth/Pentacle cards focus on everything literal and material. They put everything into a practical perspective. Earth/Pentacle cards indicate something is going on with the give-and-take on a physical level, such as money, housing, food, and work matters. They show abundance and the lack of it.

Earth/Pentacle cards may point out health issues. They also look at the structure and security that affect the situation.

Expressive-movement qualities for Earth/Pentacle cards: Contracted, courageous, fearful, greedy, grounded, insecure, lazy, organized, practical, secure, solid, steady, slow, strong, or stubborn

Astrological Earth Signs and the Body

Taurus	neck
Virgo	colon
Capricorn	knees

Ace of Earth/Pentacles

Meaning: All aces represent a new beginning. The Ace of Earth is a beginning of something tangible, a new enterprise, or a new way of receiving money. You may be starting a new job. There is a literal shift of some kind. A seed has been planted.
Expressive-movement qualities: Pure earth
Dance pace: Slow/still
Chakra: Earth/root–grounded
Physical focus: Neck, colon, and knees
Astrologic influence: Taurus, Virgo, and Capricorn
Intention: Build a strong foundation for a long-term plan.
Suggested moves and props: Joyfully and carefully pretend to plant a tree. Contemplate a disk (a Frisbee) that represents a single coin.

Two of Earth/Pentacles

Meaning: Two of Earth is harmony and change. It is juggling two equal objects, opportunities, or activities. It is yin and yang or a duality. Find the appropriate balance in whatever you are doing in due time.
Expressive-movement qualities: Earth with fire
Dance pace: Quick
Chakra: Earth/root–grounded
Physical focus: Knees
Astrologic influence: Jupiter in Capricorn makes truth, faith, and grace more expansive. It provides leadership that is moral and greatly organized.
Intention: Find the pulse between two forces.
Suggested moves and props: Shift weight of feet, hands, and shoulders back and forth. Use yin and yang symbols. Juggle two balls.

Three of Earth/Pentacles

Meaning: Three of Earth indicates a group activity. It often refers to negotiating a business deal or a way of working together, being one part of a triad, or apprentice training. Everybody involved has a role. Three of Earth portends the synthesizing of ideas into successful efforts.
Expressive-movement qualities: Earth with fire
Dance pace: Quick
Chakra: Earth/root–grounded
Physical focus: Knees
Astrologic influence: Mars in Capricorn understands what to do and how to make things work. It can produce the energy it takes to grow and evolve in a wise way.
Intention: Establish an environment to work with others as a team.
Suggested moves and props: Have others join in. Switch roles by changing hats, gestures, or other props.

Four of Earth/Pentacles

Meaning: Four of Earth indicates a structure, powerful and whole. It is stable and focused. Four of Earth also shows a protectiveness. Sometimes Four of Earth means holding on to one's self so tightly it comes across as selfish.
Expressive-movement qualities: Earth with fire
Dance pace: Quick
Chakra: Earth/root–grounded
Physical focus: Knees
Astrologic influence: The sun in Capricorn provides a solid foundation, a natural ability toward accomplishment.
Intention: Create a healthy boundary that allows for new growth.
Suggested moves and props: Make a structure out of the available materials. Sit tightly holding on to your knees, embodying being tight. Let go with long and then short release patterns. Repeat.

Five of Earth/Pentacles

Meaning: All Fives signal turning points. The Five of Earth suggests the feeling of being alone and a perceived lack of resources. It suggests a conflict, worry, or concern. The Five of Earth may caution a genuine health issue.
Expressive-movement qualities: Earth with fire
Dance pace: Slow/still
Chakra: Earth/root–grounded
Physical focus: Neck
Astrologic influence: Mars in Taurus gives us the drive, desire, and courage to get through hard times. Mars in Taurus takes its time.
Intention: You are never alone. You are guided moment by moment.
Suggested moves and props: Wearing a heavy cloak or extra layers of clothing, bend over drudgingly. Open and close eyes in amazement.

Six of Earth/Pentacles

Meaning: The Six of Earth compels us toward generosity for no particular reason. You may be drawn to give a gift or receive a gift that you didn't expect.
Expressive-movement qualities: Earth with water
Dance pace: Slow/still
Chakra: Earth/root–grounded
Physical focus: Neck
Astrologic influence: Moon in Taurus gives a sense of security. It influences us to go for what we want.
Intention: Share your resources.
Suggested moves and props: Scatter coins around the room. Then walk slowly, picking up each coin.

Seven of Earth/Pentacles

Meaning: The Seven of Earth is about waiting for things that are already set in motion to happen. It supports your progress.
Expressive-movement qualities: Earth with earth
Dance pace: Slow/still
Chakra: Earth/root—grounded
Physical focus: Neck
Astrologic influence: Saturn in Taurus helps us take responsibility and find more meaningfulness.
Intention: The reward for patience is patience.
Suggested moves and props: Wait. Look at your watch, stomp your feet, jump up and down. Do a yoga tree pose to symbolize being centered and calm.

Eight of Earth/Pentacles

Meaning: The Eight of Earth acknowledges working hard and possibly developing a skill or trade. It shows the benefits of perseverance that leads to success.
Expressive-movement qualities: Earth with fire
Dance pace: Moderate
Chakra: Earth/root—grounded
Physical focus: Lower abdomen
Astrologic influence: Sun in Virgo helps us organize and pay close attention to details. It gives us the inclination to fix what's not working properly.
Intention: The price of success is hard work.
Suggested moves and props: Act out being very busy. Practice a new move until you get it right. Express in movement the mind slowing to stillness.

Nine of Earth/Pentacles

Meaning: The Nine of Earth represents joy in the flow. The Nine of Earth signals happiness and satisfaction. It indicates reaching our full potential, being content and confident. It is maturity.
Expressive-movement qualities: Earth with earth
Dance pace: Moderate
Chakra: Earth/root—grounded
Physical focus: Lower abdomen
Astrologic influence: Venus in Virgo provides us an opportunity to slow down and access love relationships.
Intention: Embrace the delight in your life.
Suggested moves and props: Pretend to be in a well-maintained garden, smelling the flowers with satisfaction.

Ten of Earth/Pentacles

Meaning: All Tens bring us to an ending. The Ten of Earth tells us about sharing and rejoicing with family. The Ten of Earth is a completion. It usually refers to financial wealth and prosperity. It indicates the ultimate of material comforts that may come with responsibility.
Expressive-movement qualities: Earth with air
Dance pace: Moderate
Chakra: Earth/root—grounded
Physical focus: Lower abdomen
Astrologic influence: Mercury in Virgo helps you focus and be constructive and efficient. It sees the big picture.
Intention: Share your prosperity.
Suggested moves and props: Construct a completion ceremony. Give out awards.

Page of Earth/Pentacles

Meaning: Earth pages represent another person or an aspect of you that is influencing your situation by being contemplative and gaining knowledge from reading books. He/she is a hard-working student.
Expressive-movement qualities: Earth with earth
Dance pace: Slow/still
Chakra: Earth/root—grounded
Physical focus: Neck, colon (lower abdomen), and knees
Astrologic influence: All earth signs: Taurus, Virgo, and Capricorn
Intention: You will reap the rewards of your efforts.
Suggested moves and props: Use books as a prop and act as if you are studying.

Knight of Earth/Pentacles

Meaning: Earth knights are another person or an aspect of you that is influencing your situation by moving forward slowly and methodically. The Knight of Earth can support you moving ahead in any project steadily and patiently. They work hard and are committed.
Expressive-movement qualities: Earth with fire
Dance pace: Quick
Chakra: Earth/root—grounded
Physical focus: Neck, colon (lower abdomen), and knees
Astrologic influence: All earth signs: Taurus, Virgo, and Capricorn
Intention: Take charge without getting overwhelmed.
Suggested moves and props: Use a representation of a horse.

Queen of Earth/Pentacles

Meaning: Earth queens are another person or an aspect of yourself that is influencing the situation with a sense of security. She connects to us with loving kindness. The Queen of Earth is a recipient of wealth and prosperity.

Expressive-movement qualities: Earth with water

Dance pace: Moderate

Chakra: Earth/root—grounded

Physical focus: Neck, colon (lower abdomen), and knees

Astrologic influence: All earth signs: Taurus, Virgo, and Capricorn

Intention: Make healthful lifestyle choices. Look to where you can help others.

Suggested moves and props: Wear a queen's crown and robe. Use an abundance of scarves.

King of Earth/Pentacles

Meaning: Earth kings are another person or an aspect of yourself that is influencing the situation in a paternal way. He is practical and confident. He calmly takes control. The King of Earth is very reliable and is a good business authoritarian.

Expressive-movement qualities: Earth with air

Dance pace: quick

Chakra: Earth/root—grounded

Physical focus: Neck, colon (lower abdomen), and knees

Astrologic influence: All earth signs: Taurus, Virgo, and Capricorn

Intention: Be a little extravagant. Splurge.

Suggested moves and props: Walk around, with crossed arms, and pretend that you are managing others in a kind way. Wear a crown and robe.

CHAPTER XII

TAROT CARD SPREADS

Either using a *PWT* deck of another deck, *Tarot in Motion* may be used to do readings without making dances.

Questions

Instead of asking questions that can be answered with "yes" or "no" responses, consider opened-ended questions.

Suggested questions clients may ask of the cards:

What can I learn from this situation?
How can I best approach_____?
What are the implications of my choice(s)?
What are and how can I overcome negative circumstances?
Am I off-course?
What has to happen for me to reconnect to myself / another / a situation?
What is going on?[1]

Why try to figure something out when you can ask the Tarot?

One-Card Reading

Tarot in Motion most often uses pulling one card at a time, with a themed question.

Shuffle the deck and spread them out. Pull one card on a particular inquiry as a quick read or a supplement to your activities.

Why try to figure something out when you can ask the Tarot?

It is helpful, while learning the Tarot, to pick one card at the beginning of the day, then ponder the meaning and references. At the end of the day, look up the meaning. Did it make sense?

Three-Card Reading

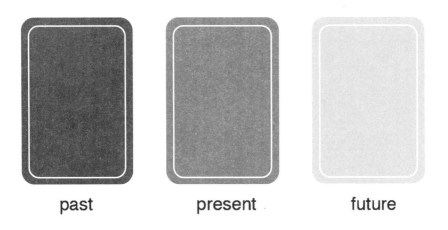

| past | present | future |

Shuffle the deck and spread out the cards.

Focus on your past, present, and future in general or on a particular issue.

Pull three cards; the first being your past, second being your present, and and third being your future.

Four-Card Reading

Focus on your question or intention.
Shuffle the deck and spread out the cards.
Pull four cards, one at a time, and place them from right to left in a row.

You may choose several sets of four for deepening or clarifying your question.
The meaning of a card is strengthened if it is in the placement that corresponds to its element.

For example: a fire card in the fire (first) placement

Weakened cards are as follows:
Water card in a fire placement
Fire card in a water placement
Earth card in an air placement
Air card in an earth placement
More than one card of the same element or number strengthens the meaning of those cards in the spread.

earth	air	water	fire

Earth	**Air**	**Water**	**Fire**
Physical	Mental	Emotional	Spiritual
Sense	Thought	Love	Create
Work	Contemplate	Relationship	Insight
Money	Ideas	Connect	Passion
Structure	Movement	Flowing	Brightness
Methodical	Speed	Receptive	Action
Organize	Disperse	Nurturing	Focus
Grounded	Lightness	Merging	Vitality

Place and read cards from right to left.

Ten-Card Reading–the Celtic Cross

The Celtic cross is probably the most popular Tarot spread. The order of how the cards are laid out and what they mean varies from reader to reader.

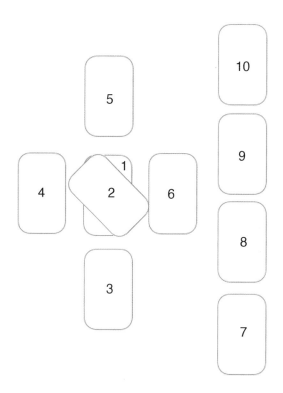

Card 1–Heart of the situation
Card 2–What crossing the situation
Card 3–What is below you
Card 4–The past
Card 5–What is above you
Card 6–The future
Card 7–You
Card 8–The environment
Card 9–Your hopes and fears
Card 10–Outcome

Pulling cards that are reversed or upside down:
Typically, reversals indicate the opposite meaning of a card. When a card is reversed, it is often interpreted as constricted or stagnant energy that needs attention.

CHAPTER XIII

EXERCISES TO INCLUDE
IN YOUR SESSIONS

The breath exercises brought total release and more grounding in a new reality.

—Linda

Guided group exercises may include breathing, physical warm-up exercises, and meditations to open up the energy channels. You do not have to follow the following suggestions precisely. If you are a facilitator, or group collaborator, incorporate whatever works for you where and when needed.

Here are a few possibilities.

Polarity Yoga Warm-Up

With your eyes closed, look inward and move your eyes up and down, right and left.

Inhale through your nostrils. Exhale through your mouth, with awareness of air passing through your body.

Roll your neck carefully in full circles. Breathe into any tight spots.

Shake and rotate your shoulders. Let your thoughts settle into clear intentions.

Feel your heart beating. Let the pulse reconnect you to your deep emotions.

Breathe fully into your rib cage and move your torso from side to side.

On your back, cradle your knees and rock side to side. Notice your spine lengthen.

Standing, step forward on one foot into a gentle lunge.

Twist your torso. Repeat on the other foot.

While seated, rest one hand on your forehead and one on your abdomen. Breathe.

Lie on your stomach, Bend your knees and cross the feet at the ankles. Reverse and repeat.

Sit on the floor, with legs extended. Roll your legs back and forth from the hip joints.

While standing, place your palms on top of your thighs. With slightly bent knees, sweep your hands downward toward your knees. Make a loud, fiery "RAM" sound.

Stand up straight. With your hands above slightly bent knees, make circles to the left and then to the right.[1]

Stand with one foot in front as if you are about to take a large step. Bend your knees. Lift up your back heel and then slowly lower it. Repeat on the other leg.

While seated, lift one foot at a time, then rotate ankle counterclockwise, then clockwise.

Stand up straight. Make contact with the earth. Feel every point of both feet evenly balanced on the ground.

Close your eyes. Lift your head up high. Allow the glow of yourself to flow through you.

Be wide awake with presence. Become aware of the cosmic forces at hand.

Sit comfortably. Become aware of the love in your heart and allow that to expand outward to all.

Dance wherever you are. Feel the joy of being alive in the beautiful, abundant world.

Heart Meditation

Keep your hands soft and relaxed. Place one hand on your heart and gently rub. Breathe and feel the quality of your breath. Place the other hand on your lower abdomen. Focus on calming the breath. Allow any scattered thoughts to dissipate. Feel your heart open.

Chakra Lineup

Sit up on a chair with your feet on the ground or stand up straight.

Imagine the four corners of each foot equally balanced on the ground.

Push up or down on any point that does not feel balanced. (If you are lying down, bend your knees so that your feet are flat on the surface, comfortably positioning your "sit bones.")

Feel the bottom of your feet as if they were solidly on the earth, growing roots that are going deep and deeper.

Become aware of energy traveling up your legs, into your ankles, calves, knees, and thighs.

Imagine this energy meeting at the base of your spine, the location of your earth chakra. Breathe in the color red.

Imagine your earth chakra spinning clockwise (clockwise is however you imagine it).

Simultaneously imagine the roots that you have established coming up from the ground.

Bring the energy from your earth chakra up to your water chakra.

Now see this chakra spinning, and imagine the color orange.

Bring the energy from your water chakra up to your fire chakra.

Now get that to spin, and imagine the color yellow.

Bring the energy from your fire chakra up to your air chakra.

Now get that to spin, and imagine the color green.

Bring the energy from your air chakra up to your ether chakra.

Now get that to spin, and imagine the color blue.

Bring your energy from the ether chakra up to your third-eye chakra.

Now get that to spin, and imagine a deep-indigo color.

Bring the energy from your third-eye chakra up to your crown chakra.

Now get that to spin, and imagine the color violet.

Reverse and repeat.

Humming Vibration

Do this lying down, sitting up, or standing or walking around. Begin to hum and send this vibration through out your body. Send the buzz of the humming into your entire body, including you bones, muscles, and cells. Experiment with changing the tone and volume of your humming. Does the sound change as you send it to different parts of your body? Try humming the sounds associated with the chakras:

Ham   Ether
Yam   Air
Ram   Fire
Vam   Water
Lam   Earth

Stop humming and close your eyes and feel the sensations in your body.

Mirroring

Mirror each other as you dance. Face your partner and take turns being the mirror. One leads and the other follows. Do your relationships mirror back to you the feeling that you understood, accepted, loved?

Body Activating

In pairs, choose persons A and B.
A follows B, walking next to or closely behind. A gently taps a body part on B (example: shoulder, fingertip, knee), who then moves, exaggerating that body part.
After a minute, A taps a different body part of B, continuing to walk until directed to change. Repeat, with B now directing A. Motion Theater class.

Walking Exercise

Begin walking in a circle. The facilitator announces the paces: slow pace, medium, or quick. The facilitator also announces pathway possibilities in a circle, square, triangle, star pattern, and spiral.

Curl-Up

Curl up in a ball while sitting or lying down. Bring your knees to your chest, bending your head down. Let go and uncurl your body.

The following dance ideas are from *7 Veils: Mystical Secrets of a Feminine Path to Enlightenment*, by Meredith Zelman Narissi.[2]

Standing Dance

Everyone sit cross-legged on the floor while the dancer stands and dances. This is a unique perspective. You look up at the dance and see her.

Photo Shop

Dance and then form a group as if posing for a photo. See the "photo" in the mirror. What do you look like to others? What is your projected group image? Does it correlate with who you think you are, and how you feel inside?

Give-and-Receive Dance

Choose a partner and take turns dancing, giving and receiving energy. Feel what it is like to give and receive when you dance . . . when you relate to another . . . when you relate to yourself . . . when you relate to God.

Dance by lying on the floor, accentuating one body part until all body parts are engaged. Like a baby discovering her body, dance until you can stand. Reimagine how it felt to discover your body, one body part at a time. You discover connections of mind and body when you were small.

Elemental/Suit Exercises

AIR/SWORD EXERCISE

Stand up straight. Shake your shoulders. Let your thoughts settle into clear intentions for the task at hand.

Place your hands on either side of your rib cage. Breathe fully and move your torso from side to side.

Place your feet shoulder width apart. Slowly lean back with arms outstretched.

Place your hands on the back of your rib cage, fingers pointed toward your spine. With awareness, exaggerate breathing in and out.

Lie on your stomach, with forehead flat on the hands. Bend the knees and cross the feet at the ankles. Reverse and repeat.

Lie on your back. Reach your legs up to the ceiling. Point your toes on one foot, leading with your big toe, and trace the letters of your name. Repeat with your other foot.

Sit on the floor, with your legs out in front of you, and lift one foot off the ground at a time. Rotate the ankle counterclockwise, then clockwise.

Stand up straight. Interlace your fingers behind your back, gently raise your arms, and slowly bend forward.

Stand up straight, placing your hands on your shoulders or keeping your arms straight. Rotate your arms in small to large circles in both directions.

Stand and slowly shrug your shoulders up and down. Roll your head gently from side to side. Let it fall forward slowly. Inhale while turning to one side. Exhale while turning to the other side. Repeat.

FIRE/WAND EXERCISE

Stand with awareness. Place your hands on your midtorso. Rub your tummy counterclockwise, then clockwise.

With your eyes closed, look inward and then move your eyes up and down as if seeing the back of your head and around each ear. Look up to the top of your head, then gently look down to your feet.

Take a look at something new. Let it sink in. Close your eyes. Re-create it in your mind's eye. Open your eyes and see how accurate you are.

Sit cross-legged with your spine straight. Rest one hand on your forehead and one on your abdomen. Close your eyes and breath deeply. Repeat with reversed hand positions.

Lie flat on your back with legs straight. Bend your knees, cradling them to the chest. Rock gently from side to side. Notice your back lengthening.

Stand with your left foot in front of the right. Slightly bend both your knees. Lift your right heel and then slowly lower it. Reverse and repeat with the left foot in front.

Stand, kneel, or sit on your heels. Exhale and bend forward while pressing your fingers on your lower ribs.

Bend your knees and slightly pitch forward at the hips. With your palms on the top of your thighs, sweep your palms downward toward your knees. Make a loud, fiery "RAM" sound.

Stand with your legs hip distance apart. Clasp your hands overhead. Swing yours arms through your legs, making a "HA" sound.

Stand and swing your arms out to the left side. Reach out to the side with the right foot. Repeat on other side. Let the limbs be relaxed like a pendulum.

WATER/CUP EXERCISE

Stand up straight. Place both your hands over your heart. Feel it beating. Let the pulse reconnect you to your deep emotions.

Stand and take a wide stance with your hands on your hips. Step forward onto your right foot into a gentle lunge. Turn your torso to face right and hold. Step back. Repeat on left side.

Stand with your feet hip distance apart and place your hands on your shoulders. Move your elbows together to the center of your body, then move them back out. Repeat several times.

Place one hand on your chest or navel. Place the first two fingers of the other hand behind your ear. Hold. Reverse and repeat.

Stand and take a wide stance. With your arms straight, slide hands down to the midthighs, while you are bending your knees. Turn your head and shoulders to one side, feeling the twist in the torso. Repeat on other side.

Sit on the floor with your legs extended in front of you. Roll your legs back and forth from your hip joints in a flowing movement, similar to windshield wipers.

Lie on your back. Cradle your knees as you rotate them counterclockwise. Repeat in a clockwise motion.

Pick up several marbles, or small rocks, with your toes. Drop them into a bowl.

Walk in an imaginary line, one foot in front of the other. Repeat, walking backward.

Massage each foot slowly. Press into any tender points.

EARTH/PENTACLE EXERCISE

Stand up straight. Allow your feet to make contact with the earth. Feel every point of both your feet evenly balanced on the ground. Slowly, with awareness, walk forward.

Stand up straight, with your feet shoulder width apart. Stretch your hands upward, reaching toward the ceiling. Shrug your shoulders up toward your ears and then down. Elongate your neck.

Stand with your legs and feet together. Place your hands just above your slightly bent knees. Make circles with the knees to the left and then to the right.

Bend your knees and come down into a low squat position. Keep your heels as flat as possible on the floor. Relax and stretch from your neck to the base of your spine. Allow your arms to cradle your knees.

Stand with feet shoulder width apart. Slowly lean back with arms outstretched. Slowly turn the head to look over and behind you. Repeat on the other side.

Roll your neck carefully in full circles. Breathe into any tight spots.

Kneel on the floor, with your arms stretched out in front of you. Rest your forehead on the floor. Let your neck and head relax. Stretch your back away from your hips.

Lie down on your back, with your knees bent and your feet flat on the floor. Gently rub your stomach in a counterclockwise motion around your navel. Reverse and rub your stomach clockwise.

Stand with your legs shoulder with apart. Slowly squat down, getting your feet as flat on the ground as possible. With your fingers, press your outer calves.

Other Exercise Possibilities

Act out cards with only your face; try dancing from lying down on your back on the floor, in various paces.

Move across the floor from each of the seven chakras.

Tell a story about a card in first person and then in third person.

Use different themed decks as inspiration and create your own structure.

Tell a story or speak in gibberish.

Walk, move, or dance, then stop and freeze in position by the music being turned off or by a bell being rung.

CHAPTER XIV

TAROT IN MOTION AS A BASIS FOR PERFORMANCE AND · COLLABORATIONS

I had been given the song "Santiago" by Gillebride MacMillan to create a dance music video. The song is about the 1,500-year-old pilgrimage path in Spain, the Compostela de Santiago.[1]

Using the Tarot in Motion system for this was an easy choice. Nine dancers, ages two to seventy, asked the cards, "What is next on my path and how will I get through the obstacles that may come before me?"

First each dancer created a solo based on their pulled cards. I then choreographed portions of those dances into a mandala, using images and movements from each person's solo, echoing each other.

It became a dance of finding and feeling support, exploring our paths of life, which matched the intent of the pilgrim in the Compostela in the song.

—*May Kesler*[2]

Tarot in Motion as a Basis for Choreography
Dances made for a performance have a better success rate if they have a universal foundation. Tarot offers that foundation and also gives personalized meaning and passion for the dancers.
Create your improvisation so it becomes a repeatable phrase.
Make one movement clear.
Add second movement.
Practice transition between first
and second movement.
Add third movement and practice transition.

Two ideas for longer collaborative workshop-style sessions

Tarot in Motion as a Basis for Meaningful Choreography and Personal Growth
(Four Days)
For all levels of dancers; from dance class fans to the highly trained

A choreographic exploration using the Tarot in Motion system, which is specifically designed for movement
A somatic approach to Tarot, deepening your understanding of yourself and how to uncover and unravel physical and emotional restrictions in your pathway
Learn how to guide yourself to change habitual movement patterns.
Learn the connection between physical and emotional patterns.
Video and show your dance with guided response.

Include these:
Polarity Wellness Tarot deck
Tarot in Motion handbook or *Tarot & the Chakras* book
Lectures
Movement–dances
Card readings
Reflection and feedback
Digital videotapes of solo and group dances

Tarot in Motion and the Five Elements (Five Days)

The five elements are based on the elements found in nature: ether, air, fire, water, and earth. The five elements govern every system in our bodies and correlate with modern science. The five elements also relate to the four Tarot suits plus the Major Arcana. Finding the connection and embracing them through movement is a powerful marriage.

Each day introduces how to incorporate a different element or Tarot suit into your life's rhythms, moving your body and spirit. Breath work, exercises, mediations, Tarot, and more will be included. Fun is essential.

You will:
gain a body understanding of the five elements;
develop an awareness of what you see, sense, and feel;
understand a deeper way to utilize the Tarot; and
have fun exploring movement in new ways.

Includes these:
Polarity Wellness Tarot deck
Tarot & the Chakras book or *Tarot in Motion* handbook
Lecture
Information on the five elements
Meditations and exercises
Dancing
Card readings
Reflection and feedback

GLOSSARY

altar: A sacred space that consists of specific items meant to invite positive energy into your life. In the context of a Tarot in Motion session, an altar is a designated area in the session space to be decorated with power objects for a specific theme or meaningful to participants.

amulet bag: A bag or pouch, often worn around the neck, that holds precious objects or mementos for protection and healing. They are often made of leather decorated with beads and paintings and are often called medicine bags. Gift small cotton bags with amulet choices of small stones and herbs.

besom broom: A magical tool used to sweep out the old and sweep prosperity and happiness back in. Brooms are made from stiff, long-stemmed weeds, including their stems left over from last year's harvest, such as fennel, willow, and scotch broom, as well as colored ribbons.

breath work: Using the rhythm of your breath to heal mind-body connections

chakras: The seven basic energy centers that line up along our spines, bridging the body to consciousness and ourselves to the world. The *Tarot in Motion* handbook refers to the original Vedic names for the chakras.

contact improv: A partnered dance that explores the skills of falling, rolling, counterbalance, and lifting, using minimal effort

corn husk dolls: Dolls made out of the husks of corn in the tradition of Native American Indians. The dolls are made as a charm to protect the home, livestock, and personal wellness of the maker and their family. They are often made during the summer harvest and the festival of Lammas.

dance: In the *Tarot in Motion* handbook, dance is used to mean any kind of intentional and purposeful movement; any type of dancing, theatrical acting, clowning, yoga, singing, or playfulness.

Dancing the Tarot: The original name for Tarot in Motion

drawing or craft projects: Some sessions may integrate drawing to help open up the creative brain, enhancing a theme to help integrate what they have experienced.

elements: As referred to in the handbook, the elements found in nature that relate to but do not always exactly line up with the Tarot suits

exalts: The placement of a planet in a particular sign where the planet is in its highest power

expressive-movement qualities: Are determined by the elements that relate to particular

Tarot suits. The elements prompt essential properties to express your dance. A secondary element or subelement is from the element that the astrological sign references for that card.

Feldenkrais method: A method that is a form of "somatic education" that is a practice, a process, and a system for self-improvement developed by Moshé Feldenkrais. "Somatic education" means that it uses movement and real-time awareness of your own body sensations to guide you toward the positive changes you seek.

garlands: A wreath of flowers and leaves, worn on the head or hung around the neck as decoration

guidelines: Structured improvisation of the possibilities to follow, associated with every card, that help you generate movement material. They help you gain a visceral understanding of the cards.

improv: Short for improvisation, an impulsive free-form dancing

Hanna somatics: Developed by Thomas Hanna, this is a direct, hands-on method for teaching voluntary, conscious control of the neuromuscular system to persons suffering involuntary muscular disorders.

maypole: A tall wooden pole used in dancing celebrations that occur on the festival of Beltane. The poles are often decorated with colorful ribbons and flowers.

methods: A series of activities; steps to follow to create your Tarot in Motion dance with a specific theme in mind.

modes: The seasonal placement; the beginning, middle, or end of the astrological signs. These are also referred to as seasonal alignments.

movement-based expressive arts: A term made popular by Anna Halprin from Tamalpa Institute's work that describes incorporating visual art and writing exercises that open up more possibilities of healing through dance.

opening and closing the space: An intentional ceremony or gestures to begin and end a sacred event, allowing spiritual energy in and then closing it out.

Polarity Therapy: A profound holistic healthcare system that balances life energy in the body. It is based on the five universal elements (ether, air, fire, water, earth) and was developed by Dr. Randolph Stone (1890–1981).
    Polarity is a practical application of understanding that everything is animated by three energy

principles that describe the way energy flows. When they do flow properly, we experience health.

Polarity Therapy gives astrological references to anatomy and aligns with the suits and the astrological references found in the Tarot. Polarity is an essential foundation to Tarot in Motion.

pull a card: A term that means a choosing card or cards from a shuffled deck with a specific inquiry or intention in mind

Rolfing®: A system of soft-tissue manipulation and movement education that organizes the whole body in gravity, developed by Ida Rolf. Rolfing bodywork affects the body's posture and structure by manipulating the myofascia system (connective tissue).

scores: Used in association with creating a dance. The concept of a score comes from a musical score. Scores are the steps to follow for making a specific dance (healing-movement pieces).

secondary element: The secondary optional element movement quality to use in a Tarot in Motion dance. It is derived from the astrological sign reference for a particular card.

Seder plate: A ritual plate used at the Passover table of ceremonial foods that are used to tell the story of the Jews' exodus from Egypt.

sessions: A broad term referring to Tarot in Motion classes, workshops, or events

smudge sticks: Small bundles of dried herbs burned as a cleansing ritual of objects or spaces. The sticks are of made up mostly of sage and may include cedar, sweetgrass, and lavender.

somatics: Translates as "of the body." The term is used in dancing, bodywork, movement studies, and psychotherapeutic practices. Somatics emphasizes connecting the external with the internal sensations. In dance, this is in contrast with "performative techniques," which emphasize the external observation of movement by an audience.

sun salutation: A sequential series of yoga poses popular in most yoga practices

symbol strips: The series of symbols in every card description. They are also on top of each *Polarity Wellness Tarot* card to guide you in creating your dance.

witnesses: The participants who are attending a Tarot in Motion group session and whom you share our dances with. Being witnessed differs from being part of an audience in that witnesses are encouraged to engage in the process. In the healing process, it is important to be seen. It is often said that you need only one witness in order to heal.

written exercises: Some sessions may integrate writing exercises to help sort out an intention for pulling cards, directions to follow a score. Writing may help reflect on what participants have experienced.

NOTES

INTRODUCTION

1. Bonnie Bainbridge Cohen, "An Introduction to Body-Mind Centering®," in *Sensing, Feeling, and Action: The Experiential Anatomy of Body-Mind Centering®*, 4th ed. (Northampton, MA: Contact Editions, 2017).

PREFACE

1. Journal article, Yvonne Owens PhD
https://www.academia.edu/35479913/THE_WITCHS_WHEEL_A_Discussion_about_Seasonal_Magic_and_Lunar_Time_in_the_Traditional_Calendar
2. Exodus 15:20–21.
3. Merce Cunningham (1919–2009), a dancer and choreographer who was in the forefront of modern dance.
4. Robert Rauschenberg (1925–2008), a painter, sculptor, and collage artist who was a pioneer of the pop art movement. He made stage sets for several modern-dance choreographers.
5. John Cage (1912–92), an avant-garde composer of music left by chance; artist and a collaborator of Merce Cunningham.
6. Lower East Side Printshop, a not-for-profit printmaking studio in New York City.
7. Miriam Jacobs, *Polarity Wellness Tarot* (Oakland, CA: Polarity Wellness, 2012).
8. Miriam Jacobs, *Tarot and the Chakras* (Atglen, PA: Schiffer, 2014).
9. Famous quote by Aristotle.
10. Anna Halprin with Rachel Kaplan, *Making Dances That Matter–Resources for Community Creativity* (Middletown, CT: Wesleyan University Press, 2019).

CHAPTER II

1. Angeles Arrien, *The Tarot Handbook* (Sonoma, CA: Tarcher Putnam, 1987), 213.
2. "Full Moon Names: Traditional Names for the New and Full Moon," https://www.almanac.com/content/full-moon-names.
3. Jacobs, 8.
4. Inspired by: Meredith Zelman Narissi, *7 Veils: Mystical Secrets of a Feminine Path to Enlightenment* (Bloomington, IN: Balboa, 2017), 80.
5. Kim Krans, *Wild Unknown Animal Spirit Deck and Guidebook* (New York: HarperCollins, 2016).
6. Jaime Sams and David Carson, *Medicine Cards* (New York: St. Martin's, 1999).
7. China Highlights, https://www.chinahighlights.com/.

CHAPTER III

1. Twyla Tharp, 1941, a dancer and choreographer, who collaborated with noteworthy artists and musicians.
2. Twyla Tharp, with Mark Reiter, *The Creative Habit: Learn It and Use It for Life* (New York: Simon & Schuster, 2003).
3. Jacobs, *Tarot of the Chakras*, xx.
4. Jacobs, *Tarot of the Chakras*, xx.

CHAPTER IV
1. https://www.Tarot.com.
2. Randolph Stone, *Dr. Randolph Stone's Polarity Therapy: The Complete Collected Works* (Sebastopol, CA: CRCS, 1986), 1:14; and Franklyn Sills, *The Polarity Process: Energy as a Healing Art* (Berkeley, CA: North Atlantic Books, 2002), 1–32.

CHAPTER V
1. Journal article and email.
2. Personal communication and email.
3. Marcela Lobos, *The Rite of the Womb*, http://theriteofthewomb.com/.
4. Lobos.
5. Personal communication, email, and Mama Donna Henes: Urban Shaman website, https://donnahenes.com/.
6. https://www.huffpost.com/entry/easter-eggs-history-origin-symbolism-tradition.
7. Personal communication, email, and dailybell website, http://dailybell2008.blogspot.com.
8. https://oakland.chapelofthechimes.com/events/summer-solstice-concert/.
9. Garden of Memory, https://www.gardenofmemory.com/.

CHAPTER VI
1. Jacobs, *Tarot and the Chakras*, 18–20.
2. Ibid., 20.
4. Ibid., 21.

CHAPTER XII
1. Jacobs, *Tarot and the Chakras*, 53.
2. Ibid., 52.

CHAPTER XIII
1. Jacobs, *Polarity Class handouts*.
2. Narissi, *7 Veils*, 60, 80, 114.
3. Jacobs, *Tarot of the Chakras*, 179–182.

CHAPTER XIV
1. "Compostela, a Dance to 'Santiago' by Gillebride MacMillan," YouTube, 2019, https://youtube/X_0jtIpyem0.
2. Personal communication and emails with May Kesler, collaborator; and Keslerdances: A Contemporary Dance Company website, https://www.keslerdances.com.
3. Personal communication and emails with Dehanna Rice, dancer, mind-body breath worker, and collaborator.

SOURCES

Anodea, Judith. *Eastern Body, Western Mind: Psychology and the Chakra System as a Path to the Self*. Berkeley, CA: Celestial Arts, 1996.

Anodea, Judith. *Wheels of Life: A User's Guide to the Chakra System*. Woodbury, MN: Llewellyn Worldwide, 1988.

Arewa, Caroline Shola. *Opening to Spirit*. London: Harper Collins, 1998.

Arrien, Angeles. *The Tarot Handbook*. Sonoma, CA: Tarcher Putnam, 1987.

Bainbridge Cohen, Bonnie. "An Introduction to Body-Mind Centering®." In *Sensing, Feeling, and Action: The Experiential Anatomy of Body-Mind Centering®*. 4th ed. Northampton, MA: Contact Editions, 2017a.

Bainbridge Cohen, Bonnie. *Sensing, Feeling and Action: The Experiential Anatomy of Body-Mind Centering®*. 4th ed. Northampton, MA: Contact Editions, 2017b.

Beaulieu, John. *Polarity Therapy Workbook*. New York: Biosonic Enterprises, 1994.

Beaulieu, Thea Keats. *Moving with the Elements: New Protocols with Sound, Affirmation and Visualization*. 2015.

Chitty, John, and Mary Louise Muller. *Easy Exercises for Health & Vitality*. Boulder, CO: Polarity, 1992.

Cullinane, MJ. *The Complete Guide Book for the Crow Tarot*. Centralia, WA: Gorham, 2019.

Greer, Mary. *Tarot for Yourself*. Franklin Lakes, NJ: New Page Books, 2002.

Halprin, Anna, with Rachel Kaplan. *Making Dances That Matter—Resources for Community Creativity*. Middletown, CT: Wesleyan University Press, 2019.

Halprin, Daria. *The Expressive Body in Life, Art and Therapy*. Philadelphia: Jessica Kingsley, 2003.

Henes, Donna. *Celestially Auspicious Occasions, Seasons, Cycles, & Celebration*. New York: Berkeley, 1996.

Janeveski, Ana, and Thomas J. Lax. *Judson Dance Theater: The Work Is Never Done*. New York: Museum of Modern Art, 2018.

Jacobs, Miriam. *Polarity Wellness Tarot*. User's guide with Stephanie Swafford. Oakland, CA: Polarity Wellness, 2012.

Jacobs, Miriam. *Tarot and the Chakras: Opening New Dimensions to Healers*. Atglen, PA: Schiffer, 2014.

Krans, Kim. *Wild Unknown Animal Spirit Deck and Guidebook*. New York: HarperCollins, 2016.

Narissi, Meredith Zelman. *7 Veils: Mystical Secrets of a Feminine Path to Enlightenment*. Bloomington, IN: Balboa, 2017.

North O'Connell, Jessica, and Yvonne Owens. *The Witches Wheel: A Discussion about Seasonal Magic and Lunar Time in the Traditional Calendar*. 2016. https://www.academia.edu/35479913/.

Pollack, Rachel. *Tarot Wisdom*. Woodbury, MN: Llewellyn Worldwide, 2009.

Sams, Jamie, and David Carson. *Medicine Cards*. New York: St. Martin's, 1999.

Sills, Franklyn. *The Polarity Process: Energy as a Healing Art*. Berkeley, CA: North Atlantic Books, 2002.

Starhawk. *The Spiral Dance: Rebirth of the Ancient Religion of the Great Goddess*. New York: Harper & Row, 1979.

Stone, Randolph. *Dr. Randolph Stone's Polarity Therapy: The Complete Collected Works*. 2 vols. Sebastopol, CA: CRCS, 1986–87. Originally published 1954–57.

Website Sources

https://www.almanac.com/
https://www.biblehub.com/
http://www.billevansdance.org/
http://www.contactimprov.com/
https://www.chinahighlights.com/
http://dailybell2008.blogspot.com/
http://www.dancefacts.net/
https://donnahenes.com/
https://feldenkrais.com/
https://gathervictoria.com/
http://www.halloween-website.com/
https://hannasomatics.com/
https://www.history.com/
https://www.huffpost.com/
https://www.iadms.org/
https://onewillowapothecaries.com/
https://ourpastimes.com/
https://www.peacefuldumpling.com/
https://www.rolf.org/
https://www.sophie-world.com/
https://www.smithsonianmag.com/
https://www.tarot.com/
http://theriteofthewomb.com/
https://www.timeanddate.com/calendar/
https://wicca.com/

Polarity Wellness Tarot: The First Somatic Deck
Cards: Miriam Jacobs & Stephanie Swafford, 2012
User's Guide: Miriam Jacobs with Stephanie Swafford

Polarity Wellness Tarot connects Tarot to Polarity Therapy. It was originally created as a tool to be incorporated along side bodywork sessions. *PWT* is the preferred deck to be used for Tarot in Motion.
Each card includes a "Polarity Man" highlighting physical focal points. At the top of each card are related symbols for chakras, elements, related astrological symbols, and types of touch. The *Tarot in Motion* handbook has translated the relational symbols of *PWT* into guidelines to create Tarot in Motion dances. Available at https://polaritywellness.com/shop/.

Tarot and the Chakras: Opening New Dimensions to Healers
by Miriam Jacobs
Schiffer Publishing, Ltd., 2014
Coalition of Visionary Resources award 2015
Tarot and the Chakras expands the information of the *PWT* deck with more-extensive card descriptions detailing attributes, advice, and stories. It supports a holistic view of the Tarot and examines various ways to alter energy systems, thereby affecting patterns presented to you in the cards. It explores the energy behind the Tarot and how it interconnects with the chakras and other systems of knowing.

Discover ways to take the messages of the Tarot a step further than Tarot alone. Get more present and mindful in your body.

Miriam Jacobs is a San Francisco Bay Area healer and dance enthusiast who has been reading Tarot cards for over 30 years. After a successful career as a visual artist in New York, Miriam found herself drawn to the healing arts. In 1994, she began formal training and was certified in Polarity Therapy. In 1996, Miriam moved to California to continue her healing-arts studies and open a private practice. As creator of *Polarity Wellness Tarot* (2012) and author of *Tarot and the Chakras* (2014), Miriam synchronizes several healing systems with Tarot to bring our experience of ourselves into heightened consciousness. Miriam now uses the cards to support others to create cathartic-movement pieces: Tarot in Motion. She focuses on safe share, process, and having fun.